The Ultimate 2021 Guide to Candlestick Charting

ALEX RICHARDS

Advanced Candlestick Charting Techniques & Strategies used for profit in Stock and Forex trading.

Table of Contents

INTRODUCTION

—— ✑ ——

The world has moved past the time when the sales of physical goods were the determiners of the world's wealth. The marketplace has become virtual so only those that are smart enough to move with the tides of time benefit from the range of opportunities that the virtual world presents to the millennial. As it stands, people make tens of millions of dollars from the comfort of their homes, but as I said, you need to be smart to tap into the goodness of modern technology in the investment world.

It should not be surprising that while a lot of people suffer the effects of the global financial crisis, others keep moving up the radar of wealth as they continue to top the charts of the world's richest people. Although it may be profitable to sell tangible or intangible goods/services, it is best for everyone in the 21st century to look beyond the ordinary and make the best of every passing minute. This is one of the reasons why day trading has become extremely popular in recent times.

Many millennials are now open to the idea of virtual trade with millions of people trading cryptocurrencies, investing in forex, day trading, and the likes. It is unfortunate, however, that while many people invest in these trades, a lot of them find themselves losing out on a chunk of their funds because they don't have the right knowledge and strategy into making the right decisions of what to buy and what best time to buy and sell to maintain profitability.

In my years as a trader who is well versed in technical analyses, I have come to realize that one of the struggles that bedevil most traders, especially the newbies and many oldies is the ability to determine what time is best to buy or sell. You see, if for instance, you buy a stock at $1000, you have to be able to make a profit from your stock whenever you decide to sell it. Unfortunately, some people find themselves selling prematurely, just a little above the amount they spent on buying, or in worst cases, sell it at a loss. How then do such people join the league of winners?

While this problem affects a lot of people and even discourages many others from investing in virtual trades, the solution isn't very far-fetched. With the right information and knowledge, everyone would benefit from day trading. One of the many ways to combat losses in this market is to get an in-depth knowledge of candlesticks as it will help you in the technical analysis of your stock.

With the candlesticks patterns and techniques that you will learn in this book, you will find yourself analyzing the market like every other expert, such that you will be able to tell what the opening and closing price of a particular stock is in a day. This will help you stay updated with trends in the market, as you won't need to rely on others (news, magazines, blogs, etc.) for information; the world is at your fingertips. When you eventually decide to sell your stock, you will do that with confidence, knowing that you are making an informed decision based on current trends and prices. This is a good way to make a profit. With time, you will find yourself among the league of smart traders who are yielding profits from day trading.

Thanks to my experience over the years and my encounter with many people who do not yet know how to monitor their market trends, I have decided to put this tell-it-all piece about candlesticks together, such that traders can learn the A-Z of candlesticks and how it can help them navigate the stock market. I have poured my expertise, knowledge, and experience into this book to make it an eyeopener for those who struggle with their stocks. You will not only learn about what candlesticks are and how they can be beneficial to your trade, but you will also get a good understanding of how candlesticks can change your trading story from that of constant struggles to one which is filled with tales of success that translates into maximum returns on your investment.

In this book, I will analyze the types of candlesticks, their patterns, the charting techniques used in this technical analysis, and lots more. I write this with confidence because these are proven techniques that I have applied over the years, and they have helped me to gather a stream of passive income.

If I must be sincere, I will tell you that my early days as a trader were not without trials and errors, but the good thing is that I was able to get a hang of these techniques. Among all the tools that I have used so far, candlesticks have proven to be very practical and straightforward. It helps you see the progression of price actions at a particular time or within a period.

As a day trader, before you go into the analysis of your daily trade, you need to understand what candlesticks really are and the best way(s) to use them. You are certainly at the right place as this book leads you through an intense but interesting technique known as candlesticks, but before we proceed, let us get you familiar with what candlesticks are.

History of Candlestick Charts

The main theories or concepts of Japanese Candlesticks came into being more than three hundred years ago, thanks to Sokyu Honma, a Japanese rice trader who lived between the years 1716 to 1803. Sokyu spent most of his life in Sakata where he was also known and referred to as Munehisa Homma. He is considered the grandfather of candlesticks because of his great works in recognizing price patterns. He is highly reputed as one who propelled the research technique that later became the foundation for Japanese trading.

He took his time to study the movement of stock prices and commodities like rice, and this helped him to spot the features and patterns of daily trading structures. He became a very wealthy man by producing a formidable trading strategy and went ahead to create a strong reputation for being diligent and veracious in trading. This he was able to achieve by tapping into his rich knowledge of rice markets and some candlestick strategies.

Sokyu made remarkable success in trading, so much so that he clinched the rank of honorary Samurai and was also appointed financial advisor to the government. He wrote a book in 1755 titled the 'Foundation of Gold- the Three Monkey Record of Money'. In this book, he described his discoveries and observations on trading psychology. Sokyu had already written his Sakata's Constitution where he explained the rules and methods, he used to gain success with his trading techniques before candlesticks became a thing.

Although there is a remarkable level of uncertainty in stock markets, candlesticks have come to be embraced by experts. It is, therefore, worthy of note that this charting technique that is now widely accepted first entered the Japanese trading arena at the advent of rice markets in 1750. Sokyu often gets all the credit for developing and honing the major principles and techniques of Japanese Candlesticks. It is very inspiring to note that Sokyu at the time when he invented Candlesticks was ways ahead of his time. To this day, he is regarded as the forerunner of this trading technique.

Another remarkable feat by this ancient trader would be the amalgam of his constitution with fresh concepts of Candlestick charts to produce what is now widely known as the Sakata's Five methods. This he did at the time when candlesticks gained more popularity. Note that his constitution and Five Methods are named after Sakata which is his place of birth.

Sokyu paid keen attention to the markets, and this helped him to gain a strong understanding of candlesticks. Little wonder he became phenomenally successful by applying candlestick techniques. As a result of his exceptional understanding of candlesticks and his deep knowledge of the rice markets, he was highly revered. He always kept records of the weather conditions every year and went ahead to analyze investors' psychology. He usually reflected on the times when rice exchange was birthed. He used his connections and the friendships he made at the time of the death of the Osaka Rice Exchange in Tokyo. Homma is reported to have made 100 winning trades at that time (Tam, 2007). Before him, no other Japanese or any other person in the world attempted to use past prices to forecast the movement of prices in the future. Interestingly, he ventured into it and did it seamlessly.

Sokyu was nicknamed Dewa's Long-nosed Goblin because of his charisma and reputation with very profitable trading methods. He was also called the god of marketers and was largely regarded as a legend. So much so that a song was composed in his honor by the Edo people (now known as Tokyo) to applaud his achievements. The song largely describes Sokyu's influence in the rice markets at that time. After he died in 1803, his books that described his trading principles became more popular and soon moved on to be the base of candlestick charting techniques that have now become so popular.

Candlesticks Versus Bar Charts

C andlesticks are the most popular amongst the charting methods for traders for many reasons. The candlestick chart is also classified as an OHLC (Open, High, Low, and Closing) chart just like every other chart that shows open, high, low, and close prices of a particular period. The interesting thing about candlestick charts, however, is that you don't need to break a sweat to get the information that you need for trading. Another OHLC chart that is used amongst traders is the bar chart which is similar to candlesticks in a lot of ways.

CANDLESTICK COMPONENTS

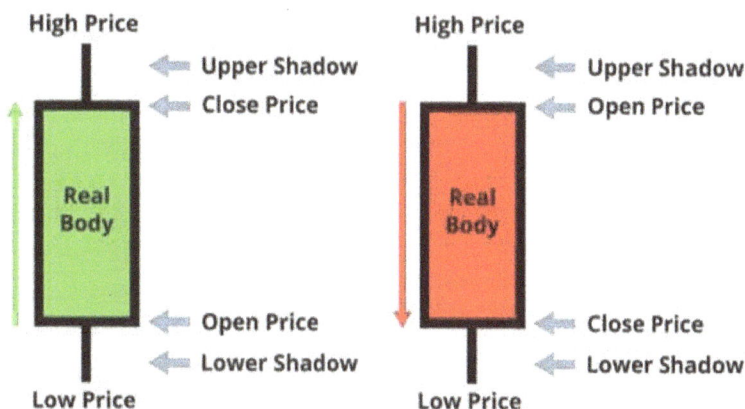

High Price

Upper Shadow
Close Price

Real Body

Open Price
Lower Shadow

Low Price

High Price

Upper Shadow
Open Price

Real Body

Close Price
Lower Shadow

Low Price

When taken in plain sight, the candlestick chart appears to be incredibly attractive as it gives a precise knowledge of the market sentiment of the period under review. Take a one hour chart for instance, which shows that the OHLC of the hour under study. If the chart is a daily chart, a single candle will be used to reflect the OHLC of that day.

The open and close in candlesticks are linked by a thick band known as the body of the candle. The high and low, on the other hand, are depicted by a very slim line that stems from the body to the end of the high or low. As you may already know, this line is known as the wick.

Bar Charts

Open - High - Low - Close Bar OHLC Bar

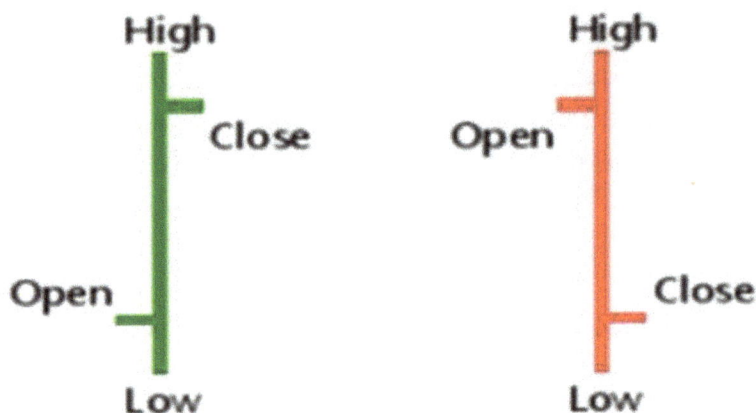

Figure 4- Source: elearnmarkets.com

This type of charting system was born in the Western world and became really popular in the early 20th century, thanks to Charles Dow's influence.

Bar charts typically display the same information as candlesticks. Every bar in a bar chart shows open, high, low, and close prices. This is why they are also known as OHLC Bars.

The truth is that bars are only graphed in a different pattern from candles. When you take them in plain sight, you will notice that they have thick vertical lines starting from the high to the low of a given timeframe. You will also notice a small horizontal hyphen on the left side which reflects the open prices, and on the right side is a small hyphen that shows closing prices.

To understand a bar chart better, remember that the bar close to the left always features the close price which is at the same level as the open price of the current bar. The bar closer to the right, on the other hand, features the same open price as the close price of the current one.

Note, however, that this may not always be the case as there may be price gaps in some markets.

When you see long vertical bars, you should immediately understand that it means that there are differences between the high and low of the time in review. This translates to an increase in the volatility of the period. Small vertical bars on the bar chart translates to minimal volatility.

When you notice a wide gap between the open and close, you should understand that there were substantial changes in prices. Another factor to consider in bar charts is the closing price goes far, higher than the opening price. In such cases, it means that there was a rush in activities from buyers at the time. This may also mean that people will buy more in future. A close that is not far from the open means that there was not any convincing change in price movements at a given period, also fewer buyers and sellers activity in the price movement indicates a correction or indecision.

The location of the close when compared to the high and low can also give you important insights. If the price of a stock appreciates during a period with a closing price that is quite below the high, it means that close to the end of the period, there was a rush of sellers into the market. This translates to lower bullish as opposed to when the asset is closed at a price close to the high price for the given period.

While bar charts may be a bit more difficult to interpret than candlesticks for some people, they also present as much information as candlesticks when it comes to the trends of the current pair.

Although for obvious reasons, candlesticks have become more popular and widely accepted by traders, it is not necessarily better than bar charts as they largely serve the same purpose. However, if you are looking for a tool that will yield you maximum returns without stress, I can assure you that candlestick is the best choice. The most important thing about any chart is its user-friendliness and usability, and that is what you get from using candlesticks. My professional advice, however, will be that if you find yourself struggling with understanding what the white body of the candlestick stands for, but you can easily grasp the use of bar charts, you should stick to bar charts. The good thing with these chart patterns is that most websites allow you to choose how you wish for your chart to be displayed and this makes it easier for you to analyze.

Chapter 1: What is Technical Analysis?

By way of a simple definition, technical analysis is a system of studying and forecasting price changes in financial markets. This system makes use of previous price movements and market surveys to predict future changes. The idea of technical analysis is hinged on the notion that once traders can figure out past market trends, they will be able to come up with an almost precise prediction for future price direction.

Technical analysis is classified under one of the two main schools of market analysis. The other school of market analysis is fundamental analysis, but while fundamental analysis is hinged on the real value of an asset as well as the meaning of external factors and intrinsic values, technical analysis focuses mainly on an asset's price chart. Technical analysis deals solely with identifying the patterns on a chart to forecast future trends.

It is correct to say that technical analysis is the umbrella term for a range of strategies that are based on the interpretation of price actions in a market. In most cases, technical analysis focuses on figuring out whether or not the market's current trend will sustain. When it shows that the trend will not last long, the question becomes, when does reversal happen? While some technical analysts use trendlines, others focus on candlesticks patterns, while others would rather use bands and boxes that are formed using mathematical visualizations. In most cases, technical analysis combines tools to forecast the possible entry and exit points of their trades. For example, the chart formation may reveal an entry point for a seller who is selling short, but the seller might wish to look at the moving averages of different periods to ensure that there is a possibility of a breakdown.

There are many ways in which a trader can analyze his trades to know whether or not an investment is good or know when to invest or sell. The general market, economic data, fundamentals, and financial statements are all factors that are beneficial and must be examined when you are looking out for a new investment- whether it is stock, forex, or any investment at all. The best way to determine a good or bad investment, however, is through technical analysis.

Unlike what is obtainable in fundamental analysis, in technical analysis factors like trends and price changes to analyze the feasibility of a future investment are considered. Technical analysis is basically the prediction of future price movements by studying the movements of the past. Just as it is with weather forecasts, technical analysis may not give you precise forecasts of future trends and prices, but it will help you gain insights into price trends that the market is likely to experience in the future.

You can apply technical analysis to futures, indices, stocks, commodities, and other tradable items where price trends are determined by elements of demand and supply. Price data or market action can be referred to as any combination of the high, low, volume, open, or close interest for a particular trade at a specific time. The timing can be either intraday (which are trades that take place in minutes or hours), daily, weekly, or monthly price data. This data may last for a few hours or wander for many years. Technical analysis typically uses different charts to reflect these price trends over a certain period.

Basics of Technical Analysis

The main principle that guides technical analysis is the fact that market prices are a reflection of every information available which is capable of influencing the market. Because of this principle, the need to study fundamental, economic, or recent developments becomes void as they are all factored into the price of a particular security. To technical analysts, the market's general psychology is that prices move according to history and trends to repeat themselves. There are two main types of technical analysis, they are technical or statistical indicators and chart patterns.

Chart patterns are a peculiar type of technical analysis that involves the identification of areas of both resistance and support on a chart by studying a particular pattern. These patterns are influenced by psychological factors, and they are fashioned to give insights into price movements, to track breakouts, or to give breakdowns from specific price points or times. If for example, you have a rising triangle chart pattern, it means buyers are losing momentum that creates a squeeze in the price. You have a bullish pattern that reflects a major area of resistance. When there is a breakout from this type of resistance, there is a possibility of an important upward price movement.

Technical indicators on the other hand are a statistical method of technical analysis that involves the application of mathematical formulas to volumes and prices. The most popular type of technical indicator is moving averages. Moving averages smoothens price data to ease the identification of trends. Simply, if the price is above the moving average, we can consider the price at buyers' territory. Similarly, if the price comes down below the moving average, we can consider it a selling opportunity.

There are other intricate technical indicators like the Moving Average Convergence Divergence (MACD). This technical indicator is used to study the relationship between many moving averages. Several trading systems use technical indicators because they can adopt the use of quantitative calculations.

You will find out that many analysts use the top-down strategy for technical analysis, and this starts with a range of market analysis, then as it proceeds, it comes down to the specifics according to the industry or sector that they wish to focus on. They then move further to analyze individual stocks which in most cases is the ultimate goal.

The good thing about technical analysis is its versatility. The principles of technical analysis are universal and can be applied the same way in any part of the world. You can adopt the same theory to the levels of technical analysis, and the best part is that you don't need some sort of special certification or degree to delve into technical analysis. A chart is a chart anywhere in the world and it really does not matter what the timeframe of the chart is or what type of security you are trying to trade. You can apply any of the core principles of technical analysis to any chart. You have to be careful though so that you won't be carried away. While it may seem as though I am making it sound so easy, you will need a lot of practice to get a grasp on any type of technical analysis. This is the only way you can yield your desired profit with it.

Key Indicators in Technical Analysis

Technical analysts make use of indicators when they seek market opportunities. While there are many indicators, volume and price-based indicators tend to be the favorite for many traders. These indicators help you decide the support and resistance levels from where the price is expected to reverse. However, when the price breaches these indicators, it provides further trading opportunities. In that case, we may consider that the price does not want to reverse, instead follow the current direction. A trader can use what is known as multiple time frame analysis to see what the price or other indicators are for a timeframe of either a second, a month, or more. This is what helps the trader to get different insights into the price action.

Below are the different types of indicators in technical analysis:

Trend Lines

Trend lines are indicators that reflect the direction of the current price by combining the low-price points using a line on the chart. The lines are especially useful, and they come in very handy for cryptocurrency traders. These lines are very useful in reflecting both long and short-term trends.

Below is a chart showing the price trend for Etherium in one year:

In this image, we can see how the price used the trendline as a helping hand. It moved higher as soon as it touched the trendline. If you were in the market with this graph, you can definitely make money by buying from the trendline zone.

The Need for Accuracy

Technical analysts that use candlestick charts have an ongoing debate as to whether or not trend lines should be taken from either the open or close of the body of candles or the high and low of the wick. The truth is that regardless of whichever method you choose to adopt, consistency remains the most important factor. You need to stay consistent with whichever method you decide to use and avoid using two different methods at the same time.

Support and Resistance Levels

Trend lines are usually confused for support and resistance levels. I have chosen to refer to the horizontal price core areas as support and resistance levels in this book. This is because trend lines are sometimes taken as areas of support and resistance.

Support levels can be determined by the fact that a good number of traders are willing to invest in security at a particular level. This is because these traders think that the security is either selling at a discount or they think that it's selling at a good price so they want to buy at that point with the belief that the price might rise soon. Resistance level on the other hand is the opposite of support level. A resistance level is a point where traders believe that there is no possibility of the price going higher, hence when the price of a security gets to the resistance level, there is a surge in supply, so the price comes back down.

The candlestick chart above shows that at the point when the price drops to a former resistance level as indicated by the red boxes, it drops back down. This is a bearish indicator that shows how difficult it is for the price to push beyond the former resistance level, so it had to fall back to the closest support.

Breakouts

A breakout happens when the price hits the former support or resistance level then breaks out by either going beyond that resistance level or falling below the support level.

Typically, after a breakout comes a rush in volume marked by bulls turning into bears or vice versa because their 'safe place' has been 'destroyed' so they are now faced with the possibility of being on the wrong side of the trade. False breakouts are also a thing. This happens when there is a sudden breakout but there isn't any change in trend so the price returns to the mean quickly, then goes back to its previous place between support and resistance.

In this image, we can see how the price broke below the support level instead of moving up. Later on, the price moved further low and came back to the breakout level again, indicating the perfect breakout and retest of the price.

Moving Averages

This is one of the tools that are most widely used in figuring out price trends at a particular time or timeframe. Moving average depends on the average price of a security for a stipulated period according to the user. If for instance, you are using a 10-period moving average on a candlestick chart that has been set to a one-day timeframe, your moving average will reflect the average price of the security for the past 10 days.

There's either the Simple Moving Average (SMA) and the Exponential Moving Average (EMA). The EMA weighs more in its calculation of price values when it comes to the recent past days than it does the days earlier.

The chart below contains a moving average of a 50 to 200 period set at 240 minutes (four hours). When you study the chart, you will notice how the averages can be used to track market trends. The simple technique of buying when the short-term moving average which is 50 goes beyond the long-term moving average which is 200 would possibly result in making a substantial move.

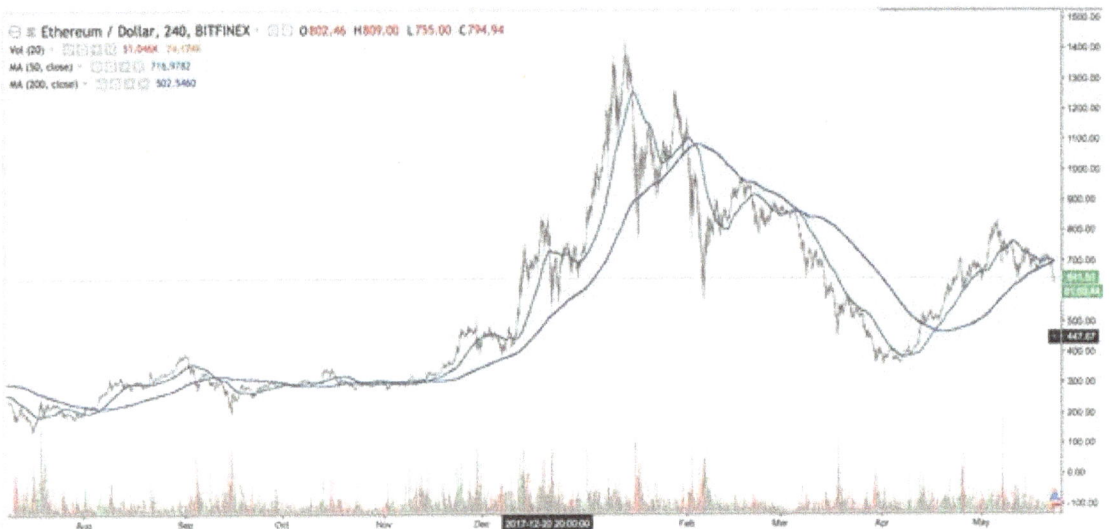

Trading Volume

Trading volume is quite different from the other indicators that I have described so far. It stands out from the others which are centered around price. Trading volume on the other hand indicates volume which is the reflection of the number of buying and selling orders that take place within a certain period. This is an especially important indicator as it goes hand in hand with price movement. When there is a large price movement, it is typically followed by high trading volumes. In the same light, consolidation periods are accompanied by low volumes. Therefore, a strong movement with the support of volume is considered as a high probable movement.

A surge in volume is typically a valuable reflection of trend reversals. The chart below shows that there were rises in sell volume at two different points at the end of both trends. These spikes were marked at the base of the move.

Technical Analysis Myths Debunked

Some traders and investors are quick to talk down on technical analysis as "shallow" chart patterns that do not have exact, ultimate, or important advantages. Other traders consider technical analysis as the 'Holy Grail' of investing. They believe that once they start using charts, they will automatically start making profits. These notions, however, have led so many people to the wrong use of technical analysis.

Technical analysis seems too controversial for many traders as they are quick to discard it as a system that does not add any value to their trade. While these types of traders exist, many others have come to believe in the efficacy of this system. It is important to note that the common misconceptions stem from those that use fundamental analysis as they tend to be very careful when they are faced with technical analysis. The real truth about technical analysis, therefore, is that many traders use it correctly and have for many years made profits with it.

Here are some myths and facts about technical analysis:

- Technical analysis is only useful for short term or day trading: this is a very common myth among investors. They tend to believe that technical analysis will only be efficacious to those who are into short-term or computer-based trading/day trading. This isn't in any way true because as it has come to be known over the years, investors and long-term traders can also use technical analysis to get desired results from periodical charts which may be either weekly or monthly. Moreover, there are many successful investors who focus on technical analysis in long term investment.

- Technical analysis is fast and easy: you are bound to come across many online courses on technical analysis and chances are that instructors will promise you 100% success. This isn't always the case, so you need to be careful who you listen to. Many people go into trading with the belief that they can make their first trade by relying solely on technical indicators. Well, while this isn't impossible, you need to be careful going forward as you will need a combination of factors like good knowledge, continuous practice, discipline, and money management skills to continue making profits. To get the best of technical analysis, you need to put in your time, attention, and knowledge. Always bear in mind that technical analysis is just a piece of the puzzle, it is just another tool amongst others.

- Technical analysis is only useful to some traders: technical analysis doesn't discriminate. Know this and know peace… if you are among those who believe that technical analysis is for traders who are into personal trading, it is time to change that mindset. Investment banks have a special trade team that uses technical analysis. High-frequency stock traders also make very good use of technical analysis. There is literally no limit to the type of trade where technical analysis can be used.

- There are automatic technical analysis software that can help traders make profits: this is another false assumption about technical analysis. You will see many internet ads for software ranging from cheap to expensive ones that claim to analyze everything for you. There are also cases where beginners mistake tools for technical analysis in broker-developed trading software for trading models that will help them make profits. You need to know that while technical analysis software can give you the right information about patterns and price trends, it doesn't mean that it guarantees success or profits. The right interpretation of the provided trends and data is what gives profit.

- Technical analysis amounts to low success: for very many years, traders have tried to debunk this persistent myth. Traders who use technical analysis have for many decades and centuries made huge profits from the right use of technical analysis and chart patterns. It is, therefore, baseless for anyone to claim that technical analysis gives low success.

- Technical analysis makes very precise price predictions: many beginners hope to get totally accurate insights from charts or software patterns. A new trader may, for example, hope to get a prediction that is as accurate as this: "stock XYZ will climb up to $75 in three weeks." An experienced trader on the other hand will try to stay away from quoting specific prices as much as possible. They would rather quote a range like, "a security might move between $40 to & $59 within the next three weeks to two months." This is why it is always advised that those who place bets according to technical insights should take note of the fact that technical analysis only provides probable ranges as opposed to specific numbers. It is generally believed that when something works very often, although it may not work all the time, such things may still be highly effective when it comes to profit generation.

- Technical analysis can automatically take the place of a good trader: artificial intelligence and technology are designed to ease processes and make them faster and more seamless. They cannot always take the place of human instincts. Before you can evaluate trends, you'll need to conduct research, have a good understanding, and possess analytical skills. Technology will only give you the support you need for accuracy, but you cannot rely solely on it when you are dealing with the equity market. This is because you stand a chance of losing huge sums if you don't monitor your stocks properly. You need to match your human instincts with technological predictions to get the desired success in technical analysis.

- Technical analysis should have higher winning rates: many people tend to believe that they need a high level of winning trades before they can make profits. Many people tend to believe that if Samuel makes four winning trades out of five, while Juliet makes one winning trade out of five, then Samuel is automatically a more successful trader than Juliet. This is not entirely true. We can't say for sure who made more profit until we can get the details. When you structure your trade properly, you'll be able to make adequate profits even when you have few winning trades. Profit levels depend on win rates and risk or reward. If Samuel made a total of $20 on his wins but lost $60 0n his losses, it means he has $0 gain at the end of the day. If Juliet on the other hand made $60 on her win and lost a total of $20 on her losses, it means she has a profit of $40 at the end of the day. In this case, it means she was more successful than Samuel who had more wins.

Strategies for Technical Analysis

As a trader, you should first have in mind that there are no magic or shortcuts in technical analysis. This means that it is impossible to get a method that will forecast all market variables.

The market moves by itself and there is a little effect of retail traders. You need to be able to figure things out yourself. Another mindset you need to rid yourself of is that technical analysis will open you up to an easy way to wealth. You'll be disappointed if you have this mindset. You need to be able to look at and analyze charts to get the best out of the technical analysis.

To build your technical analysis strategy, you need to find the right way to approach your charts. There are two ways to do this: the bottom-up approach and the top-down approach. In most cases, you'll find short-term traders applying the top-down approach, while long-term traders fancy the bottom-up approach. Once you have figured this out, you can then proceed with the other steps.

Bottom-Up Approach

This is an approach that is centered on single stocks, as opposed to looking at it from a macroeconomic point of view. A bottom-up approach includes analyzing those stocks that look viable for possible entry and exit points. If for example, an investor finds a stock that isn't quite valued in a downtrend, with the aid of technical analysis, it is possible to find a particular entry point for the time when the stock would bottom out. Technical analysts typically look for value in every step they take and seek to look at the long-term possibilities in their trades.

Top-Down Approach

Unlike the bottom-up approach, the top-down approach adopts a microeconomic analysis by looking at the entire economy before looking at every single stock or security. Traders pay attention to the economy first before they turn their sights on sectors, then they move to the companies in situations where they are selling stocks. In this case, traders look at the short-term profits and not the long-term gains. Traders who take this approach will, for example, focus on those stocks that broke out of their 20-day moving average as a chance to buy.

Below are some basic strategies for technical analysis:

Identify trends: if you want to delve into technical analysis, the first step that is expected of you is the identification of market trends. This is because before you can interpret charts like candlesticks, you need to look at past trends. The most important step to take is to look out for the strong trends that are climbing up the chart rapidly. This is where your key indicators come in handy. This is what will help you to come up with a trading system. As a beginner, you might want to stick to the moving average crossover technique. This technique allows you to keep track of two moving averages at the same time on a single price movement of a stock.

Let's have a look at a basic example of a trend.

Price is moving up= Uptrend

Here we can see that the price is moving up by creating new highs. Therefore, we can consider the trend as an uptrend. It is very easy to spot with open eyes by just looking at the chart!

Moreover, further price direction comes from the speed of the price. The slower speed indicates that the opposite party may enter and the price may reverse. On the other hand, a strong impulsive movement indicates a continuation of the current trend.

Spot securities: you should understand that the above strategy doesn't apply to every stock or securities as it is most suitable for liquid and unstable stocks as opposed to solid or stable stocks. You may need to apply different strategies to different stocks or securities according to their nature as they typically have different moving averages.

Look out for the right brokerage: you need an appropriate trading account that will bolster your choice of security. This trading account should give you the right features to allow you to track and monitor your choice of key indicators. They shouldn't cost so much so that they won't eat up a chunk of your profits. You should typically look out for a basic account that has moving averages on candlestick charts.

Keep an eye on your trades: you will need to be very active, although this varies according to the strategy you have chosen to adopt. If you are into day trading, for example, you will need to have a margin account that will grant you access to Level II quotes as well as visible market markers. According to the previous strategy, you might also have to stick to a basic account to keep the costs minimal. All that matters is for you to choose a strategy that will allow you to monitor your trades as best as you can.

Get additional tools or software's: you need many other features to boost your performance in technical analysis. You may want to get mobile alerts, or you might want to be able to track your trades on the go, or you may choose to rely on automated trading software's to trade on your behalf. Depending on your needs, you should consider getting software's that can make your work faster and seamless.

Risk Management Strategies

Risk management is what helps you to mitigate against losses in your trading career. It will also help to guard your account against total loss of funds. Basically, you want to try as best as you can to not lose funds for any reason at all. If you can manage risks, you will make more money in the market and achieve your trading goals.

Although many traders tend to ignore this especially important trading requirement, I advise that you take it seriously. While you may have the right strategies in place and may seem to be making a lot of profits, you might lose it all if you do not have the right risk management strategy in place. Remember that risk management distinguishes the major difference between the successful and unsuccessful traders. A good trader always knows how to manage trades and keep him safe from unexpected market movements. Below are some ways to guard against risks in the market:

Set appropriate expectations: if you are new to trading, you may believe that it only takes one good deal to make it big in the market. You need to be careful; what you need is a lot of work, energy, and experience. You will have to invest years into trading before you can become an authority. This is not to make you feel like trading is a herculean venture, but while the market has some unrivalled thrills, you need to have realistic expectations and concrete trading plans in place.

First off, you need to learn the basics of trading. Consider it as a profitable but very risky venture. Try to prep yourself by taking your time to learn in a safe space before you get exposed to the dangers of the market. This safe space might be books like this one, or resources on the internet. Once you have the right chunk of knowledge, you'll be able to match it up with experience and meet your goals with time.

Practice the one-percent rule: many traders have come to love the one-percent rule which encourages traders to not invest more than 1% of their capital or their trading account into one trade. This means that if a trader has $5,000 in his/her trading account, the trader should not put in more than $50 in a single trade.

This is an immensely popular strategy for traders that have less than $100,000 in their accounts. Those who have high amounts in their accounts can afford to go as high as 2%, but that means they can afford to. Some traders with large amounts in their accounts may also choose to invest lower percentages. This is a smart move because the more you have in your account, the higher your position becomes. The best thing to always do to make sure that your position remains in check is to stick to less than 2%. If you invest more than 2%, you will be at risk of losing a large sum from your trading account.

Stay away from break-even stops: you should never play yourself into the risky game of pushing the stop loss to the entry point. It might backfire as it might open you up to a range of problems. The best thing to do at all times is to keep your position safe.

This is very applicable to those who are using common technical analysis tools like chart patterns, moving averages, support and resistance, highs and lows, etc. Your entry point is never hidden and for many traders, there will be similar entry points. Experienced traders are well aware of this so the prices often fall back and crush on the inexperienced traders that stick to open price levels before the price goes back to its original trend. When you move your stop too early, break-even stops will be left out of trades that carry profits.

Calculate your expected returns: you must set stop-losses and take-profit points to be able to calculate possible returns. This calculation is very important because it causes traders to ponder on their trades and find all the rationale behind them before going into it. It also presents them with a technical way to weigh different trades and pick the ones with the most profit. You can calculate your expected profit with this formula: [(Probability of Gain) x (Take Profit % Gain)] + [(Probability of Loss) x (Stop-Loss % Loss)] (Kuepper, 2021).

With this calculation, the trader can hope to get returns on investment. The trader will in turn weigh these returns against other openings to decide which stocks to buy or sell.

Avoid fixed stop distances: you will come across many market strategies that will advise you to use fixed amounts of points or pips on stop losses, then place profit orders across various instruments as well as even markets. This is one of the shortcuts that I mentioned earlier in this section. Their shortcoming is in the fact that they absolutely forget that prices make natural movements and financial markets won't work the way they think they will.

The market's momentum and dynamics are always changing so the amount of price movements in a day, as well as its fluctuations, varies at different points. If you notice high volatility, you are expected to place your stop loss and welcome bigger profit orders. This will help you to stay away from early stop runs and increase profits whenever prices swing more. When there is low volatility, you are expected to place your orders close to the entry point and not be too excited about it.

Also, when you buy or sell with fixed distances, you won't be able to pick a reasonable price level and you will also lose the flexibility you require as a trader. You have to endeavor to always know about crucial price levels and barriers like round figures, Fibonacci levels, large moving averages, or just support and resistance.

Technical Analysis vs Fundamental Analysis

When it comes to market analysis, you will come across two schools of thought that deals with the process of market analysis. These are technical and fundamental analysis. While these two methods of analysis deal with the market, they adopt different approaches when it comes to measuring the value of a trade or investment. Both methods have entirely different components that make them attractive to individual market analysts. You, therefore, need to understand the main difference between both techniques to be able to decide which of them suits your goals more and to be able to use it effectively.

When we talk of fundamental analysis, we refer to the process that involves an in-depth examination of those factors that influence the industry, company, as well as the economy's interest. It is used to weigh the main value of a stock/security by taking the economic, financial as well as other factors into consideration. This can be either qualitative or quantitative factors that can point out openings where the value of a security change from what it currently is.

Fundamental analysis examines every factor that can influence the rate or value of a security. These factors can be based on an organization or a macroeconomic factor. The factors that influence the value of a security in fundamental analysis are known as fundamentals. They are, however, either financial statement, business concepts, competition, management, etc. The main aim of fundamental analysis is to analyze the entire economy, the business environment, the industry where it operates, as well as the firm.

This type of analysis is based on the assumption that the fundamentals are responsible for some sort of delay that has influenced the price of securities. This means that the price of securities in the short term don't correlate with their value, but in the long run, the prices adjust themselves. There are three phases involved in technical analysis, they are the economy, industry, and the company.

On the other hand, the main aim of the technical analysis is to anticipate the price movement based on past movement. Moreover, investors use multiple calculations and price behavior to predict the future movement. Unlike Fundamental analysis, technical analysis requires nothing but the trading chart.

Chapter 2: An Introduction to Candlestick Charting

From the previous section of this book, you may already have an idea of what candlesticks are and why they are important to the success of your trade. To get a clear understanding of this charting technique, we need to first understand the concept by giving it a clear definition.

What is a Candlestick Chart?

Candlesticks are similar to bar charts, but they are not to be mistaken for bar charts. The term candlestick can be defined as a technical tool that gathers data for different times into blocks of price bars. They are more explicit than the usual open-high or low-close bars because they are used to create patterns that allow traders to anticipate price trends for a given period. Candlestick charts are used to tell the story of stock prices at a particular time. This tool which can be traced back to the 18th-century Japanese rice traders employs the use of adequate color coding to make its analysis easier to interpret. When you look at candlesticks in terms of aesthetics and the presentation of data, they represent a clearer view of the price that helps traders to predict the future direction of the market. Candlestick charts are quite different from other charts, and they are way more exceptional.

Candlesticks simply present you with a clear knowledge of current or recent trading psychology. You do not need to study too hard to get a grasp on this charting technique. With little practice and some getting-used-to, you will find that you have mastered the use of candlesticks in your market analysis.

Let's have a look at practical example of how candlestick charts represent investors psychology:

Here we can see the daily chart of AUDUSD where on day 1 the price started moving lower from 0.7676 and on day 6 it closed at 0.7598. It is very easy to spot that in 6 days the price moved lower by 78 pips.

Now look, what happened on the 7th day?

The price became very strong and recovered from a 6 day loss in just 1 day. What does it mean?

It means there was less activity in the price in the last 6 days but on the 7th day, buyers became very strong. As a result, the price moved higher in the following days.

Candlesticks have become extremely popular for their ability to delineate and control many disruptions that always occur in the market. The constant external influences on stocks and future market analysis are also mitigated with this technique of market analysis. If you successfully master the use of candlesticks charting in your market analysis, it will become almost impossible for you to fancy the use of the normal bar chart.

Candlesticks is a strong tool for technical analysis, It helps to analyze the effects of trading patterns without necessarily looking for the cause. It is important to note that stock prices are always influenced by the investors' psychologically influenced emotions which manifest in either fear, hope, or greed. It is quite impossible to capture the general psychology of the market with statistics because the changes that occur in the psychological factors of the market require some sort of technical analysis. Candlesticks successfully identify and analyze the difference or changes in the general interpretation of values by investors. Beyond being a technical indicator tool, it also indicates mostly accurate price direction on forming candlestick patterns to highlight the relationships between buyers and sellers.

This tool gives insight into financial markets that may not be available when you use other charting tools. This tool for technical analysis is more efficient with commodities or stocks and when merged with some analysis techniques like candlepower and candlestick filtering, your analysis and timing skills will become perfect.

Features of a Candlestick

Before we proceed, I would like us to run through the major components of candlestick charts as I believe that this will further help us understand the role of candlesticks in technical analysis. There are three main features of candlestick charts, they are:

- The size or length of the entire candle
- The relationship between open and close
- The shadows and link to the body of the candle.

Size and Length of the Entire Candle

You are going to come across candles that open low, close high or those that are exceptionally long. When there is a downturn, these candles show that there is a major change in the market trend. If, on the other hand, there is a long upturn and if there's an aberrant long candle that closes, there will be a long shadow at the top to reflect this change. This may also manifest in the form of a long bearish body at the top. Such cases are referred to as exhaustion or a blow-off-top condition.

The body of the candlestick is the main part of the chart that reflects the difference between the opening and closing price for a particular time. It is, therefore, important for you to understand and accurately interpret the message contained in the candle from its length and size.

The Relationship Between Open and Close

When there is a solid upturn in trends, there will be a surge in open buying. Prices typically rise at such times, forming a hollow white or green candle. The length between the open and close are, therefore, reflected by the dominance of the controlling factors of such trends, e.g., the bulls.

There is also another phenomenon known as the bearish market condition, which is marked by strong downward trends. In such cases, the candle's body turns dark or red, and this shows that sellers are trooping into the market on the open and that they are dominating at a certain time. With the shape and color of the body, you will be able to predict the condition of the market at that time.

The Shadows and Link to the Body of the Candle

The length of the shadows represents what was the highest and lowest level of the price between the opening and closing time. This may also show the market's refusal of a resistance or support level. If you see the price to fall as a long downtrend and form a candle with a long wick downside, it means sellers were rejected at the wick area and buyers may enter the price any time. This typically shows the possibility of the trend exhausting itself. It also shows that the demand for the stock has increased or that the availability of the stock has reduced.

When shadows or tails form above the main body of the candle, especially following a sustained rise in prices, it means that the demand is getting low and that the supply has increased. When you notice that the shadow appears to be large, note that you need to critically analyze it closely with the main body because it might be an indication of the potency of the reversal. The pins are usually the most potent.

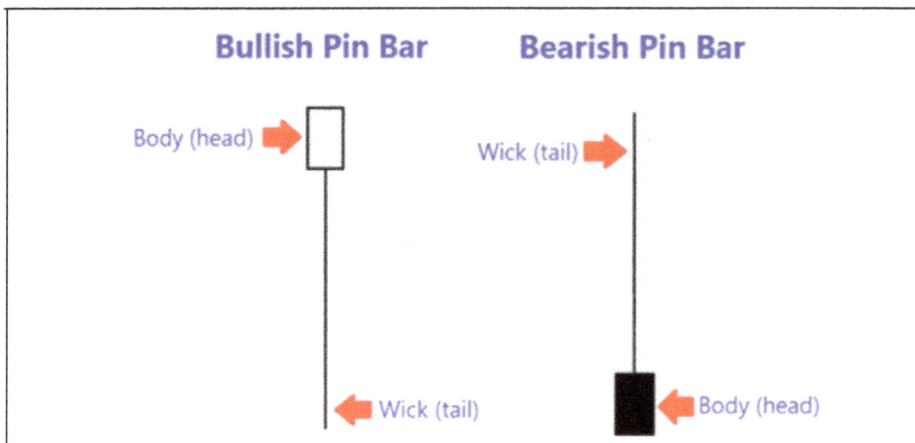

Figure 1: Source: admiralmarkets.com

The above illustration shows that the tail of the Bullish pin bar leans downward, neglecting support. This is shown by the bullish pin. There is going to be a surge of momentary buyers afterwards, and as a result, there will be an increase in price. In the same light, when the bar tail of the bearish pin leans upward and rejects resistance, there's usually a rush of momentary sellers, and this typically leads to a price reduction. The most potent reversal candles have shadows that are longer than their bodies. They may either come with a small nose or without one.

Understanding Bullish and Bearish Candle

When the opening price of the candle is above the closing price, it is known as a bearish candle. It is an indication that sellers became strong after opening the candle that pushes the price down. Similarly, when the closing price of the candle is above the opening price, it is known as a bullish candle. It is an indication that buyers became strong after opening the candle that pushes the price up. When the traded stock closes at a lower price than the opening price for a certain period, the body of the candlestick will either fill up or turn black. In this case, the closing price will be found at the bottom of the body, while the opening price will be at the top of the body.

Here we can see the visual representation of a simple bullish and bearish candle:

Opening Price

Closing Price

Closing Price

Opening Price

Bearish Candle   **Bullish Candle**

It is not unusual to find modern candlestick charts that have different colors. In modern candlestick charts, the white or black color of the body is now replaced with other colors like green, red or blue. Traders that use electronic mobile platforms have the choice of choosing between these colors.

As a beginner, it is important to understand that the body of the candlestick stands for the opening and closing prices of a traded stock within a period. This makes it easier for you to see the price range of the stock for that period at a glance. The use of colors, however, makes it easy for you to know if the prices of the stock are rising or falling.

Let's say you are studying a candlestick chart for one month; you need to first understand that each candle stands for a day's trade. If the candle then has more reds popping up than other colors, you should be able to tell that the price of the stock is falling.

The vertical lines at the top or bottom of the chart are either called wicks or shadows. These are the lines that represent the highs or lows of the price of a traded stock. Let's look at it this way: if the top shadow on a red candle appears short, it means that the stock opened at a point close to the day's high. If, on the other hand, the upper wick on a green candle appears short, it means that the closing price of the stock is close to the day's high.

Here we can see how the wicks looks like with the candlesticks

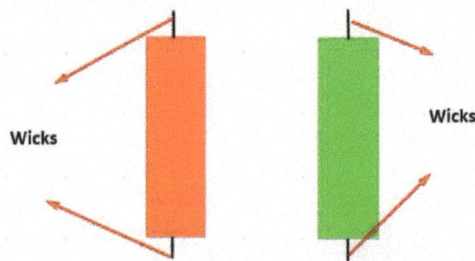

The bottom line is that candlestick charts are designed to show the link between the high and low, as well as the opening and closing prices of a stock. Note that the body of a modern candlestick chart may either be green or red, short or long. The shadows may be short or long as well. When you combine these features, you'll get the market's sentiment towards the stock.

Chapter 3: How to Read Candlestick Charts

———————— ∞ ————————

Japanese candlesticks have been embraced by traders for their potency in giving details and precise information about price changes and movements. They give graphical information about the demand and supply chain at every point in the time action.

There are three major components of a candlestick chart. They are the upper and lower shadows, as well as the body. Every candlestick on a chart stands for a particular period and the data presented by the candlestick is a summary of trades that take place during the period under review. If you are studying a 15-minute candle, for instance, what you'll get is 15 minutes of trade information. On every candlestick, you'll see four data points which are open, close, high and low. The open represents the first trade that took place in a certain period while the close stands for the last trade that occurred in that period. This is what is considered the body of the candle. Another variable to consider is high which is the most priced trade, and low which is the cheapest trade for the period under review.

Every candlestick has a nucleus or a middle point that illustrates the gap between the open and close of a stock that's up for trade. This is the part that is commonly referred to as the body. The upper reflection is the price gap between the high of the trading period and the top part of the body. The lower shadow, on the other hand, illustrates the price gap between the bottom part of the body and the low point of the trading period. It is the closing price of the traded stock that determines whether the candlestick is bullish or bearish (you'll learn about them later in this chapter). The actual body of a candlestick typically turns green whenever the candlestick closes at a higher price than the opening price. In such cases, the closing price can be found at the top of the actual body, while the opening price will be somewhere at the bottom.

Bullish Candle

High

Close

Open

Low

Bearish Candle

High

Open

Close

Low

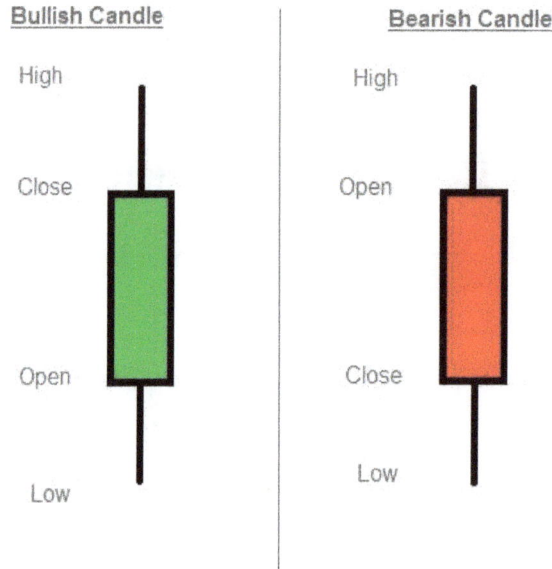

Colors are very important in candlestick analysis. The color of the body is what determines whether the price movement of the candlestick is either bearish or bullish. Different software makes use of different colors but you are most likely to come across the red, green, black or white colors. When the opening price falls below the closing price, the body of the candlestick turns green. If the green body sustains for a long time, it gets more bullish. A green body that sustains for too long is a reflection of a rush in buying (greed) during that time. What it means at the end is that the bulls won.

An opening price that is higher than the closing price on the other hand makes the body of the candlestick turn red. A sustained black body means the candlestick is bearish. If the candlestick also remains red for too long, it shows that there was a rush in selling which is usually as a result of fear at that time and eventually, the bears won. Candlestick Anatomy

When you study the features of a candlestick chart, you'll get enough insights into the following:

- The direction of the market
- You will be able to tell if the movement was linear or not, that is, if it has a tail or wick which suggests that the movement was a nonlinear one.
- The open and close price
- The highest and lowest prices during the time under study

- Location on the candlestick pattern.
- Previous candlestick patterns

It is possible to set the desired time frame for your chart as this will make the reading and interpretation of the most important parts of your trade easy. In most cases, you'll find that people prefer to have their candlestick chart ready whenever they want to make orders. The best thing to do, however, is to begin your day, week or trading session by studying time frames of longer periods. This is what is known as the multi-timeframe analysis. This analysis gives traders insights into important levels of resistance, support and the entire market trend. Take a trader who uses a 15-minute candlestick chart for example, but to get a clearer picture of the long-term market sentiment, he studies the previous day or a one-hour chart.

A candle can give you insights into whether or not a trading session closed bearish or bullish when you study it. This depends solely on the opening or closing prices. A closing price that is higher than the opening price simply means a bullish session, while it is called bearish if the closing price falls below the opening price. Remember that the upper and lower shadows always stand for the high and low prices of a particular time.

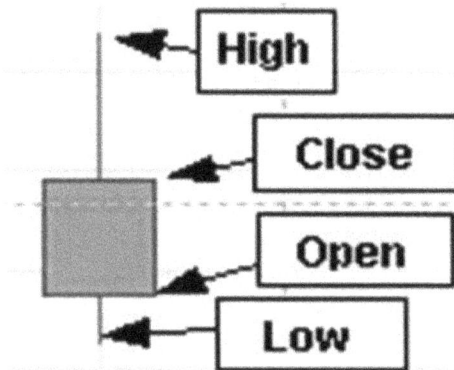

Generally, every candlestick on a chart stands for the OHLC variables. The point of the opening price, either high or low can be attained in a candle session. The point where the price closes at the termination of a period under review is an important part of your interpretation of a candlestick chart.

Open Price

The open price will be found either at the top or the bottom of the body of the candle. This depends on either an upward movement of the price of a security or a downward movement during the time under review. If there is an upward movement of price, the candlestick will turn green or white, then the open price moves to the bottom. A downward movement on the other hand makes the candlestick turn red or black. In this case, the price of the asset moves to the top. Remember that the closing price of the last candle and the opening price of the current candle will be the same.

High Price

When the price rises in a candlestick period, the high price reflects either at the top of the shadow or by the tail, just at the top of the body. Typically, there would not be an upper shadow when an asset opens or closes at the highest price. Low Price

This price either sits at the base of the shadow or the tail, underneath the body. When an asset opens or closes at its lowest price, the lower shadow disappears.

Close Price

This is simply the last price that was traded during a candlestick period. This price is shown either at the top of the body when the candle turns green or white or at the bottom of the body when the candle is red or black.

Candles continue to change according to market price movements. While the open remains the same till the candle completes its circle, both the high and low prices keep changing. As the candlestick forms, so does the color change as well. The color may move from red to green if the current price is lower than the open price, then rise above it. The last price at the end of the timeframe of the candle is the close price.

This means that the candle has been completed, so a new candle now begins to form.

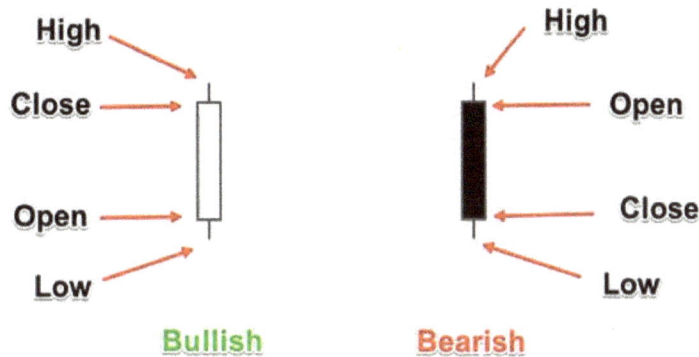

Here we can see how the OHCL formed in both bullish and bearish candle. Here, the long wick upside and downside indicates the highest and lowest price of a trading session.

Price Direction

When analyzing a candlestick chart, it is possible to see the movement of the price of an asset during a particular time frame. This movement is depicted by the position and color of the candlestick. A green candlestick means that the price closes higher than the opening price so the candle moves above, to sit at the right side of the preceding candle. A red candlestick on the other hand means that the price of the asset closes lower than the opening price so the candle falls below the previous one, also to the right side except if it is shorter than the previous one, and if it has a different color.

Price Range

The price range is the gap between the bottom of the lower shadow and the top of the upper shadow. This reflects the distance between price movement during the time of the candle chart. To calculate the range, you should minus the low price from the high.

As the world evolved, so were different candlestick patterns developed according to price movements in history. As a trader, you are expected to take quality time to study and understand these patterns because it gives you great knowledge and insights into reading market charts generally. By understanding candlestick patterns, you'll be able to understand and translate different price actions in the market, then predict the direction of future price movements of a particular stock or asset.

Although there are many patterns, we are going to discuss the most potent and commonly used ones for interpreting price charts like every other technical analysis professional.

Bullish and Bearish Candlestick Patterns

As a technical analyst, you should be able to tell how candlestick charts are characterized by different identifiable patterns. These patterns all have descriptive names. Some of the names you'll come across are the dark cloud cover, the morning star, three white soldiers, hammer, and the abandoned baby. These are just a few of the many types of candlesticks. These patterns come into being within one to four weeks and they provide traders with valuable knowledge of the future price of an asset, or the possible price movement of the said asset. Before we look at the bullish candlestick pattern, let's first take a look at a couple of principles.

1. Bullish reversal patterns come to life during downtrends else it is a continuation pattern, not a bullish pattern.

2. In most cases, bullish reversal patterns need bullish confirmation. What this means is that the pattern must be accompanied by an upward movement in prices. This can be a result of a "long hollow candlestick or a gap up" (Marianna, 2021) which is then followed by a rise in trading volume. Bullish confirmation is typically studied during the first three days of the pattern.

3. Bullish reversal patterns from a significant support or resistance followed by a trend often provides a reliable price direction. In that case, a close of the candle and the correction of the price provides precise direction.

If you require more buying pressure confirmation for the bullish reversal pattern, you can employ the use of some typical technical analysis techniques like momentum, trend lines, volume indicators, or oscillators. The truth is that there are many candlestick patterns that reflect buying opportunities. These types of patterns typically give the most solid reversal signals.

The Bearish candlestick is achieved when the opening price is higher than the closing price. The role of this candlestick is to indicate a drop in prices. Typically, the color of the bearish candlestick is red. In other words, a candlestick pattern is bearish when the opening price is lower than the closing price.

At the beginning and end of a charting period, a series of candlestick arranges in sequence close to each other. This is how the candlestick chart is formed. So depending on the opening and closing price of an asset, a candlestick may either be bullish or bearish.

The Bullish and Bearish Engulfing Patterns

The main goal of using a candlestick chart is to gain insights into market trends. There is, however, something called the engulfing pattern, which points out the possible changes in market trends. In a bullish engulfing pattern, you will notice changes in market trends as a result of downward to upward trends. In the same light, the bearish engulfing pattern shows changes in market trends which stem from an upward to a downward trend. A bullish engulfing candlestick pattern is birthed by situations when large bull candles wrap the former, after a significantly small bear candle. The bullish engulfing points that seller were dominating the market and taking the price down. Suddenly bulls appeared and engulfed bears sentiment, pointing out that the price may move higher, violating bear sentiment. The role of this pattern is to reflect changes in market sentiments rising from the bearish to the bullish pattern. This is why it is seen as a pointer to changes in market trends.

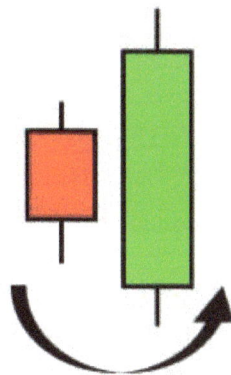

Bullish engulfing
pattern

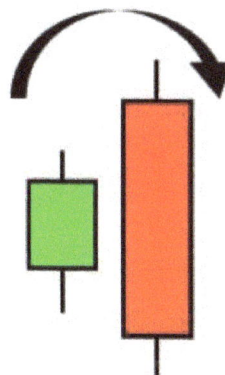

Bearish engulfing
pattern

It is of utmost importance that you should take note of where the engulfing patterns are located as relates to the entire price trend. When you study your chart, you will see that whenever the patterns are at the edges of the price trend, they seem to be headed towards the next location of the price trend.

In a nutshell, when the price goes lower, but the chart forecasts a higher price trend it means a bullish engulfing pattern. The bearish engulfing candle is the direct opposite of the bullish candle. This means when the price is higher, but the chart forecasts a lower price trend.

When you see a two-candle pattern, note that the first candle is typically the down candle while the second candle is usually the "larger up candle" (Cory, 2020) which is characterized by an actual body that completely engulfs the small down candle.

Bullish Candlestick Patterns:

Candlestick Pattern	Direction
Hammer	Bullish (Reversal)
Morning Star	Bullish (Reversal)
Bullish Harami	Bullish (Reversal)
Bullish Engulfing	Bullish (Reversal)
Long Wicks	Bullish/Bearish (Reversal)
Doji	Bullish/Bearish (Indecision)
Inside Bars	Bullish (Continuation)
Piercing Pattern	Bullish (Reversal)

Bearish Candlestick Patterns:

Candlestick Pattern	Direction
Doji	Bearish/Bullish (Indecision)
Evening Star	Bearish (Reversal)
Bullish Harami	Bullish (Reversal)
Bearish Engulfing	Bearish (Reversal)
Shooting Star	Bearish Reversal
Dark Cloud Cover	Bearish (Reversal)
Long Wicks	Bearish/Bullish (Reversal)
Inside Bars	Bearish/Bullish (Continuation)

Chapter 4: Candlestick Chart Patterns: How to Spot Profitable Patterns

———— ∽ ————

We understand that choosing from hundreds of trading opportunities can be so overwhelming. There are many available options to choose from, and this is due to several factors influencing the market. With candlestick patterns, you can get a clear picture and highlight trading signs and signals of future price movements.

Day trading patterns are used to decipher the many options and motivations, ranging from the hope of gain, the fear of loss to stop-loss triggers, short-covering, tax, consequence, and hedging, among others.

If you want to engage in day trading, it is important that you know the main components of a candle, the benefit, the two main categories of price movement, how to spot a profitable pattern, and the common mistakes newbies make. All these and more are what we will cover in his chapter. Your ultimate goal is to understand the best patterns to support your trading style. But first, let's look at the history behind the candlestick chart pattern.

Understanding candle patterns is quite technical but isn't as difficult as it seems. It is just like knowing your family members. If you have some of your relatives dispersed in a crowd of strangers, spotting them won't be easy, and you can easily miss them. But if your relatives are brought together and arranged by units, spotting them would be easy, even if they get mixed with the crowd again.

See candlesticks as relatives that can be grouped together and identified in family groups. Candlesticks can be cousins or related. Some may seem odd, but in perspective, they will blend in. The odd ones will still be remembered if placed in a family. As candlesticks form, they show the current price, whether it is moving up or going down over the time frame and the price range covered by the asset at that time.

There are four data points to every candlestick, and they include open (the opening price), low (the lowest price over a fixed period), high (the highest time over a fixed period), and close (the closing price). The diagram below is a visual representation of the data points.

Candlestick Chart Patterns

A candlestick chart pattern is used in predicting the future direction of a price. It is a technical tool that merges data into single bars at a given time. Despite being technical, the patterns are straightforward to interpret, and they can help you get a competitive advantage in an overwhelming market.

Each candlestick tells a story of the face-off between buyers and sellers, supply and demand, the bulls and bears, fear and greed. Note, many candle patterns require confirmation regarding the context of the previous candles and the future candle.

Trading beginners tend to make the mistake of identifying a single candle formation without considering the context. For instance, a hammer candle stands for a near-term capitulation bottom when the candle forms after three preceding bearing candles. On the other hand, hammer candles forming on 'flat' sideways candles are not useful. Not familiar with the hammer candles? Not to worry, we'll get to that shortly.

Basically, understanding the 'story' represented by each candle will help you achieve a strong knowledge of the candlestick chart patterns mechanism. The pattern trends always repeat themselves. However, the market tends to constantly fake out traders similarly when the context is overlooked.

Looking at the coloring of the bodies of candlestick charts, you will realize that more emotions are represented. Therefore, it is important to ensure they are well incorporated with other indicators to get the best outcome.

Benefits of Using Candlestick Patterns

The best thing to happen to any trader is to "see" the market clearly; this is why traders continuously seek ways to do this. After knowing what candlesticks patterns are, it is also important to know the benefits they offer to traders.

Are you wondering what candlesticks have to offer that other high-low bar charts don't offer?

Here they are:

Candlestick patterns are easy to understand: Candlesticks are easy-to-understand and clear patterns that are very accurate when predicting the market. Using candlesticks together with some elementary technical analysis allows you to clearly see patterns that are emerging in the market. The importance of this tool is that you take advantage and utilize the patterns in the market when trading.

Unlike other trading patterns, candlesticks do not require long months or even years before it is mastered. If you practice constantly, you can even memorize the patterns quickly. Although some sort of effort is required to memorize it, a the end of the day, you will realize that the profit potential understanding the chart brings is immeasurably valuable.

Candlestick patterns are superior to the traditional charts: The traditional charts come with little meaning, while the candlestick chart patterns show the action happening in the market in a more detailed way. Studying the price action in equity over time makes you utilize pattern analysis to know the probability of the equity's future movement. With practice and getting yourself familiar with it, candlestick chart pattern analysis can play a crucial role in most investment methods.

It is a psychological portrait: You should understand that prices are mostly influenced by hope, fear, and greed. To understand the changing psychological factors, some form of technical analysis should be utilized. Meanwhile, candlesticks enable you to read the changes in the market's determination of value, known as investor sentiment. This is done by displaying actions between buyers and sellers (this is often shown in the price movement). Therefore, a candlestick chart gives an insight into the financial markets, and this isn't so with traditional bar charts.

It has proven to be dependable for 250 years: Yes! For 250 years now, candlestick charts have proven to be dependable by helping traders know and understand market price action. Homma, who is the father of candlesticks, analyzed years of rice prices and compared them with weather conditions of each year, and in the long run, rose to become a legend in the rice trading industry. Candlesticks evolved from his trading method, and for 250 years now, we have been benefiting from the outstanding analytical tool of Homma.

It can help you identify market patterns faster: With candlestick patterns, you can easily see high probable bearish or bullish reversal patterns which other charts will not show.

With candlestick patterns, you can easily determine the current state of the market by just looking: When you look at the length and color of a candlestick, you can instantly see if the market is becoming bearish (weak) or bullish (strengthening).

You can use candlesticks for various assets: Candlesticks can be used for assets such as stocks, indices, or forex and other technical indicators such as Pivot Points or Bollinger Bands.

Newbie Mistakes that you Must Avoid

Candlestick patterns are an easy way to plan the prices of your chart. However, the fact that candlestick patterns are popular does not mean everyone uses them in the right way. Below are common mistakes newbies make when using candlestick patterns.

Newbies tend to trade candlestick patterns in isolation: Newbies do this a lot, and this can be a dangerous approach as a trader. For instance, if you look at a chart and see a Bullish hammer, you might feel it's the best time to buy, especially since the information you've read in books and online says that seeing a hammer means you are in control and you should go ahead and buy.

But do you know that shouldn't be the case? The truth is, seeing a bullish hammer means that you are in control, but it is only *momentarily*. It also does not mean that there is a high probability for the market to go up. The reason for this is, you still have to look at the context of the market and also market conditions. Acting blindly might cause great loss.

For better understanding, let us look at this explanation.

If you notice that the market is in a downward trend for the last 200 candles, and as a result, making lower lows and lower highs steadily, what are your chances of having that one hammer win against the last 200 bearish candles? Don't you think the odds are quite slim here?

Let's look at it this way… if a car with 70km speed per hour moves towards a train with 250km speed per hour, what do you think will happen to the car? Of course, it will crash and get damaged. This is exactly what happens when you buy into a tiny hammer that is in a downtrend. You will consistently get stopped out of your trade, and it isn't strategic to trade candlestick patterns in isolation.

The patterns are not set-up or signals but are there to just show what happened over the previous candle. In financial trading, traders anticipate the price direction based on probabilities. Although Candlesticks are a high probable price indicator, they are not ultimate. Therefore, the ultimate result depends on when and how you are implementing these tools in the market.

Newbies often chase the market: As a newbie trader, if you look at the chart and notice a big bullish momentum, what comes to your mind? Do you see a bullish market and picture how favorable the market will be if you buy?

If you buy after the price has moved high, you will likely face an obstacle, and that is where you need to put your stop loss. You do not have any swing low, price structure, or support to reference for your stop loss to be set. There is a high chance that you will randomly set a stop loss on your chart, which can be 50 pip or anything you feel like. The deal-breaker here is that the market has no business with where your stop-loss is.

With the huge progression the price has made, it will need to take a breather, allowing the price to either retrace or reverse. What do you think will happen then? Another trader will take profit from your stop loss while you get stopped out of your trade. This makes it so dangerous, hence it must be avoided at all costs. If you notice a huge move with the price, you have spotted a strong signal suggesting that you shouldn't be entering a trade. However, it might be too late since the energy has already been expended there.

Newbies memorize different candlestick patterns blindly: We have so many variations of candlestick patterns. In fact, there are hundreds of them out there. An attempt to memorize the patterns, their names, and meaning will have you burnt out, except in a situation where you have a photographic memory. For us without that type of memory, we will get frustrated memorizing these. But is memorizing them important?

Well, you don't need to memorize candlestick patterns; you just need to ask yourself what the market is trying to tell you. You can do this by asking yourself two valid questions we will discuss below.

What is the price range at which the candlestick closed?

We all know that a candlestick pattern has both low and high. Instead of memorizing patterns blindly, ask yourself if the price is closed to the highs. If it does, then the buyers are in control temporarily. If it closes near the middle of the range, then it might be undecided as sellers and buyers are on an equal footing. If the price closes near the lows, then it means that sellers are in control of the market.

Based on your time frame, what is the length of the current candlestick pattern compared to the previous ones?

The reason for this question is because you need to know the conviction behind the move. For instance, if you spot a hammer, and its size is almost the same as the last five candles, or maybe smaller than them, then this means there is no conviction behind the hammer. Alternatively, if you have another hammer being formed and it is two or three times bigger than the preceding candles, then this means that there is a strong price rejection and also a conviction supporting the move.

Asking yourself these two questions and figuring out the answers is how you read candlestick patterns instead of memorizing blindly. You would want to analyze the pattern size relative to the earlier candles.

Candlesticks patterns are fascinating to market players, as it captures their attention. However, several reversal and continuation signals emitted don't work reliably in the modern electronic environment. Luckily, some statistics show unusual accuracy for the narrow selection of the patterns. This gives traders an opportunity to actionable buy and sell signals.

Chapter 5: How to Spot Profitable Patterns Using Candlestick Charting

Y̲ou understand what candlestick patterns are already, now you want to take the knowledge a step further by finding out how you can spot profitable patterns when trading with candlestick patterns.

Candlestick patterns are divided into two broad groups: the bearish and the bullish patterns. These patterns indicate trend reversal or continuation of a lasting trend. Also, it is important to note that candlestick patterns are created with the support of one or more candles.

The graph below shows a cryptocurrency trade pattern with the bullish and bearish flag.

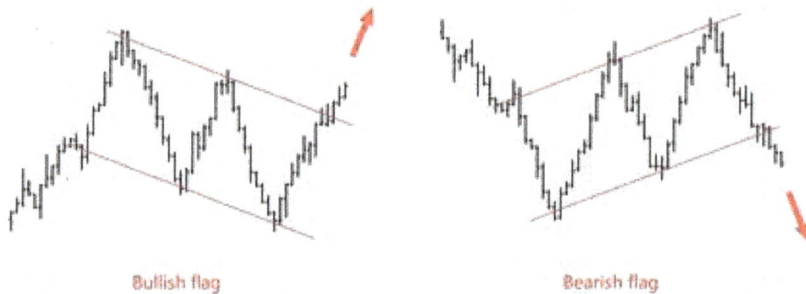

Bullish flag   Bearish flag

Bar financial data graph

Now, let's take a look at the common candlestick patterns and how to spot them when trading.

Inside Bar Candlestick Pattern

This is a candlestick pattern that signals a low volatility time in the market. This pattern suggests that there aren't many orders entering the market. Both the bears and bulls are staying calm while waiting for any development in the market.

Spotting the bar patterns in your charts is quite easy. It is a candle where the low of the inside bar pattern is higher than that of the previous candle, and the high of the inside bar pattern is lower than the previous candle high. The whole body of the candle remains within the previous candle. Therefore, the inside bar candle is at the inside range of the previous candle:

Inside Bar

Inside bar indicates:

Indecision: Since the market participants are not sure of the market direction, the market doesn't make any new lows and highs.

Consolidation: Here, the market takes a break before going towards the direction as indicated by the inside bar pattern breakout direction.

When trading with an inside bar pattern, there is a generated entry signal as price breaks through the low or high of an inside bar pattern. The breakout direction influences the trade's direction that should be opened. A bullish signal will be generated when a price breaks through the high of an inside bar, and a bearish signal is generated when it goes the opposite way. This means you can trade inside bars by setting the stop pending orders.

The other side of the candle should have a stop-loss. So, in a bullish breakout, there should be an opening of long order above the high of the inside bar, and below the low of the inside bar should have the stop-loss. The opposite should be done in a case of a bearish breakout.

Buy Here

If you have your orders stopped too soon when trading with inside bars, you should try out supports and resistances for placing stop-losses on your trade. This can be used effectively for also placing Profit-Targets.

For the body of the inside bars, it doesn't matter if it is much of a bearish, bullish, or neutral. Although, if the direction of the breakout of an inside bar is the same as the inside bar body's direction, some extra points can be added.

If you trade inside bars in the main trend's direction or if you use it together with support and resistance, there is a high chance for you to greatly increase the possibility of successful inside bar signals and take out the fake breakouts.

Inside Bar System

An image below demonstrates the profitability of the inside bar bouncing near the red rising channel. Only the bullish breakouts will be taken here.

With inside bars, you should place stop-loss orders below the rising S/R zone and above their high, place buy stop orders.

How do you know where to take profits?

The market should inform you with all you need to know, including the profits it will offer you.

Finally, you need to apply what you have learnt by opening your charts now and analyze the inside bar patterns, the main trend of the market, support and resistance, and explore how trading with an inside bar pattern will give you some really nice profits.

Pin Bar Pattern

This is an immensely popular candlestick pattern many traders use to trade successfully worldwide. A great benefit of using the pin bar pattern is linked with its versatility and recorded success rate.

Spotting profitable pin bar patterns can be done quickly and in long-term charts. The stronger the pin bar is the higher your chance of success. Some of the tools they use include psychological levels, trend analysis, significant support and resistance, moving average being used as a moving S/R, important market highs and lows, and other Forex indicators.

The pin bar pattern shares similarity with the shooting star candlestick pattern where there is a signal in the change of a bullish trend to bearish, and also the hammer candlestick pattern, where there is a signal in the change of a bearish trend to a bullish trend.

A pin bar laying and bouncing from an important support/resistance zone has a valid entry signal. Lets discuss it below:

Entries: Once the valid signal shows, that's a signal for you to enter a trade by placing the stop pending order. With a bullish pin bar, you should place the buy stop order above the high of the pin bar. While the sell stop order is positioned below the low of the pin bar, in the case of a bearish pin bar.

Stop-Loss: This should be positioned in the opposite direction of your entry point. If you are trading based on the bearish pin bar, then your stop-loss should be positioned above the high of the pin bar, while the stop-loss should be positioned below the low of the pin bar if you have a bullish pin bar. Following this rule will help and support you to adapt to the vitality of the current market.

Profit-Targets: The nearest S/R zones should be used when planning your profit-target levels and in closing trades in a profit. You can either choose to close the trade partially or close the entire trade and set profit-target levels at other S/R zones for higher profits. The profit-target for buy trades should be set below S/R zones, and during short trades, the profit-target level should be placed above S/R zones to increase the probability of profit-target getting filled.

Besides the candlestick patterns we have discussed above, there are still other patterns you can use in spotting profitable trade. They include:

Piercing Line

The piercing line is a two-masted plan that is created by a long red candle. This pattern is followed by a long green pattern and is needed to close into the previous candle, with at least 50%. Generally, the opening price of the green candle and the closing price of the first candle has a gap. This pattern will appear when a strong buying pressure enters the market after a fall in price. You can interchange this pattern vice versa with a bearish pattern.

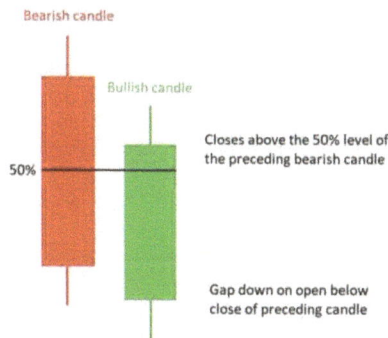

Morning Star

The morning start is a pattern that signals a reversal. It consists of three sticks with a short body candle between a long red body and a long green body, which is the bullish version, or it can go sideways (in the bearish version).

Three White Horse

This pattern takes place with three candlesticks. It is a long white or green repeated candle with small wicks. It progressively opens and closes higher than the previous candle. If it appears, it is indicating a powerful bullish signal taking place following a low character trend, displaying a steady advance of the buying pressure. The pattern also indicates a low selling pressure and an existing bull market on the horizon.

Hanging Man

The hanging man is a fascinating and interesting pattern. It looks exactly like the hammer or pin bar, but with a little difference; it appears in an uptrend and not during a downtrend. This pattern indicates a huge selling during the day (in its continuation version). If buyers were able to raise the price again, it signals a continuation of the current trend.

Note, the hanging man is a continuation pattern, while the pin bar is a reversal pattern.

We have several and many more effective and profitable candlesticks out there. You can learn more if you want. However, I have shared the ones I use personally in this chapter, and I hope you use them in your profitable trading too.

Chapter 6: High Probability Bullish Candlestick Patterns

Bullish candlesticks stand at the base of all stock charts as the most important pattern. By now, you should already have a clear idea of what bullish candlesticks are, but if you are still unclear about the meaning and importance of this very profitable pattern, I'll take my time to reiterate what they are. A bullish candlestick appears on the chart when traders cause prices of security to go up. It usually results in a higher close price than the opening price. A bullish candle is either white or green on the chart.

Bullish patterns usually form following a downtrend market. Their appearance suggests a change/reversal in price movements. With this, traders become aware of the chance to go into a long position for profit from the upward trend.

Bullish reversal patterns are, however, the candlestick patterns that show that prices are about to change direction or reverse. These are some of the most profitable patterns in a chart and they are usually used to confirm positive signals for traders' technical strategies. Simply put, bullish reversal candlestick patterns show you that a previous or ongoing downtrend is about to end and may change to an uptrend. When the candlestick pattern is bullish, it reflects in either a single or multiple candlestick patterns.

Note, however, that bullish reversal patterns typically appear following a downtrend, else it is merely a continuation pattern. Also, it is especially important to confirm that the reversal signals you see are bullish. This can be done by studying other variables like the trading volume.

Another important type of bullish candlestick is the engulfing candlestick pattern which presents the opportunity to go into a trend at a good time. A combination of the trend and the engulfing candle as a call to action is a very great bullish strategy.

Just as you might already know, every trader wants the market to remain a bull market at all times, but this isn't always the case. To make for a balance in the market, the bull market has to go to rest for the bear market to take over and it is this time that everything gets set for traders to take their next big move. Just as it is with plants or even animals, they cannot continue to bear fruits round the clock. This is why winter makes for a perfect time for relaxation for trees. If trees must be fruitful in the next season, there must be enough cold during winter for them to relax. In the same light, the bearish trends in the stock market have the same effect on the market as winter has on trees. The more relaxation time there is for the bearish market, the stronger, and better will the profits be when the trend reverses to the bullish market.

At this point, you might want to ask what are those bullish reversal patterns (or signals) to look out for? First, let's get to know how to read these patterns.

How To Read Bullish Chart Patterns

Your first point of consideration in reading any candlestick pattern is that every candlestick chart reflects 24 hours' worth of price data which includes the opening and closing price, as well as the high and low of that day. By the color of the body of the candlestick, you should be able to tell whether the opening price is higher than the closing price. You can use this formula for any time-bound chart you wish to analyze. You should also understand that there is a possibility of using a candlestick chart ranging from 1-minute candles to monthly candles.

To further confirm a bullish candlestick pattern, you can apply different features of technical analysis like momentum, volume indicators, trend lines, or oscillators. This will make it easier for you to confirm the buying pressure during a reversal. The truth is that various bullish candlestick patterns suggest buying opportunities, just as many bullish stock patterns reflect strong reversal signals.

When it comes to bullish engulfing candles, they are made of two candles, the first of which is made up of a small body and short shadows. The second of the bullish engulfing candle is characterized by longer wicks and a bigger body that submerges (engulfs) the body of the previous candle.

Before you can say that a pattern is a bullish engulfing pattern, the high of the second candle must climb higher than the high of the former candle. The same goes for the low.

Typically, the closing price which is reflected at the top of the body should be more than the highest point of the wick of the previous candle. This gives more importance to the second candle and indicates that the bulls are now in control of the market's price action.

Types of High Probability Bullish Candlestick Patterns

Hammer Candlestick Pattern

A bullish hammer can be described as a lone candle that stays within the price chart to reflect a bullish reversal. It is quite different from the other candlestick patterns in the sense that it is a single candle that projects a change during an already existing downtrend.

The hammer candlestick pattern is so-called because of its shape which looks like a hammer. The lower wick of this candlestick pattern is two times higher than the size of the actual body. The body of the hammer candlestick, however, reflects the distance between the opening and closing prices. The shadow, on the other hand, reflects the high and low prices of a given period.

Bullish Hammer

Take a close look at the picture above. To interpret the hammer candle, you must understand the open, close, low and high levels of the hammer. The price of the security must sell-off, such that a new low is created for a particular currency pair to create a hammer. After this price drop, the rates must show signs that sellers failed to hold the momentum and buyers took the price near the opening level

Significantly, a trader must always bear in mind that bullish hammers need wicks that are at least two times higher than the entire candle body. Also, the candle must in itself either turn red or green based on how strong the reversal is.

In many cases, the bullish hammer is mistaken for the bearish hanging man candle. This misidentification is not surprising as the two candles look the same. The difference between the two candles, however, is their position in a market trend. Although the hanging man is characterized by a long wick and a small body, it is usually hanging at the end of an upward trend. Bullish hammers, on the other hand, are characterized by a small body, long wick, but placed at the end of a downward trend.

What Does the Hammer Candlestick Say?

After a security decline for a while, the hammer appears to indicate that the market is struggling with determining a bottom. Hammers point possible resolve by sellers to form a base coupled with a price rise to reflect a potential reversal in price trend. This usually takes place within the same period when there is a fall in prices after the open, only for it to gain more strength, then close around the opening price.

The most effective hammers are those that come after at about three or more declining candles. You might want to ask what a declining candle is? This is a candle that closes at a lower price than the close of the preceding candle.

Typically, a hammer looks like a 'T' so when such appears on your chart, you should anticipate a hammer candle. A hammer candlestick wouldn't reflect a reversal in an uptrend until it's confirmed. This confirmation is done when the hammer closes higher than the closing price of the hammer. This confirmation candle is typically a reflection of strong buying. This is when traders are expected to take either long positions or exit short positions. Those who are entering fresh long positions require a stop loss below the hammer shadow's low.

It isn't very common to use hammers independently, even after confirmation. Traders usually make use of either trend analysis or price or other features of technical analysis to further confirm this candlestick pattern. There is no specific time for hammers to occur. They might appear in one-minute charts, daily or weekly charts.

The Inverted Hammer

The inverted hammer pattern, also known as the inverse hammer is a type of candlestick that surfaces on a chart due to pressure from buyers to cause the asset's price to spring up. This pattern is always at the base of a downward trend, pointing at a possible bullish reversal.

The name inverted hammer is inspired by the shape of the pattern which looks like a hammer that's turned upside-down. This hammer candle is characterized by a small body, a short lower wick, a long upper wick.

When an inverted hammer forms after a long downtrend, it is bullish because prices at that time don't go down fast during the day. Sellers typically cause prices to return to their initial open position, but the increase in prices reflect the test by the bulls on the strength of the bears.

What Does the Inverted Hammer Say?

The inverted hammer is simply an indication of a bullish reversal following a downtrend. This signal is an awareness that bears have failed, and the bulls are now ready to buy securities at the fallen rates. Following a downtrend, buyers exert pressure on the market for a rise in stock prices.

At this point, the sellers are aware of the need to exit because a bullish reversal might follow. In the same light, the buyers are also aware of the need to enter their buying position because the inverted hammer indicated the beginning of a bullish trend. Just as it is with the hammer, do not forget to use other technical features to confirm the signals or simply wait for the following trading day for the confirmation of the start of a bullish trend. If the opening price of the next trading day/session is higher than the closing price shown in the inverted hammer candlestick, then it is time to enter a buy position.

Bullish Engulfing Pattern

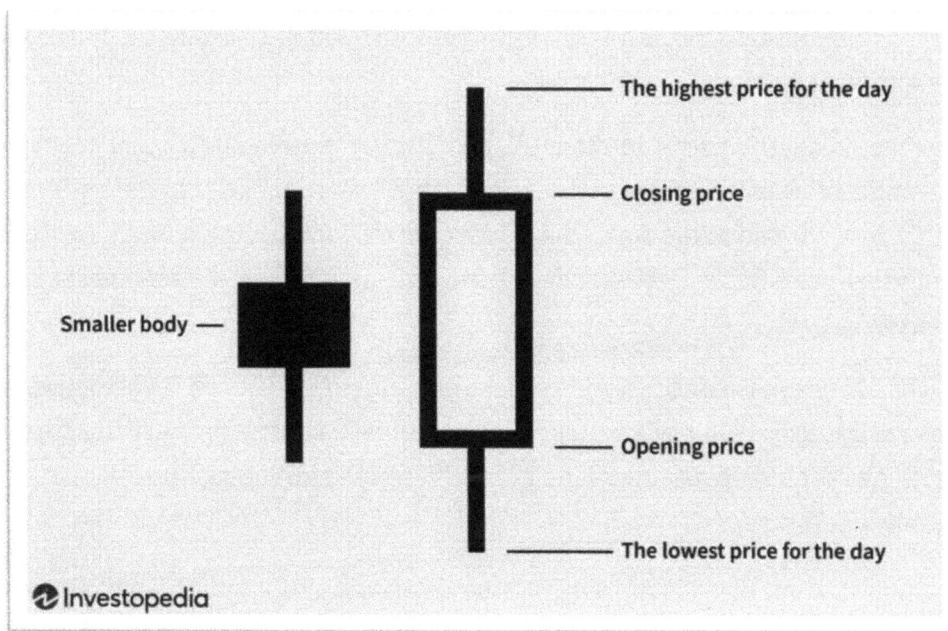

A bullish engulfing candlestick pattern is a trend reversal pattern that indicates the possible end of a downtrend. It shows the change in trend and a projected end to a downtrend. This pattern shows that there will be a change in trends, followed by an uptrend. Just as the name implies, the pattern is characterized by two candles where the engulfing one completely overshadows the preceding candle. Simply put, the preceding candle is totally contained by the range of the engulfing candle, from the low to the high. Usually, the first candle is the red or black candle, while the second is the green or white candle.

The green or white candle pops up immediately after the initial candle. This is the bullish candle, and it is usually longer than the preceding bearish candle. The opening price of this candle is usually lower than the initial closing price but closes higher than the former opening price. It completely engulfs that black or red candle.

What Does The Bullish Engulfing Candle Say?

You shouldn't make the mistake of interpreting the bullish engulfing candle simply as a white or green candlestick that stands for an uptrend after the black or red candlestick which reflects a downtrend. Before the formation of a bullish engulfing candlestick pattern, there must be low opening prices on the second market day compared to the closing price on the first market day. If the price of securities does not go down, then the body of the white or green candlestick wouldn't possibly engulf the body of the black candlestick from the preceding trading day.

The white candlestick seen in the bullish engulfing pattern shows that the bears had control over the price of a security in the morning but lost this control to the bulls who took over from then at the end of the day. This is based on the fact that the security opened lower than the closing price of the previous day, but closes higher than the opening price of the previous day,

The white or green candlestick seen in a bullish engulfing pattern is characterized by a small upper wick, that's if it has any upper wick at all. What this tells you is that the market closes at, or close to the highest possible price. This points to the fact that the day's trades ended during an uptrend.

The absence of an upper wick supports the possibility of another white/green candle the next day which will close at a higher price than the close of the bullish engulfing pattern, even though there is a possibility of a black or red candlestick the next day after a wide gap at the opening. This candlestick pattern often enjoys a lot of attention from technical analysts because it indicates trend reversals.

Piercing Line Candlestick Pattern

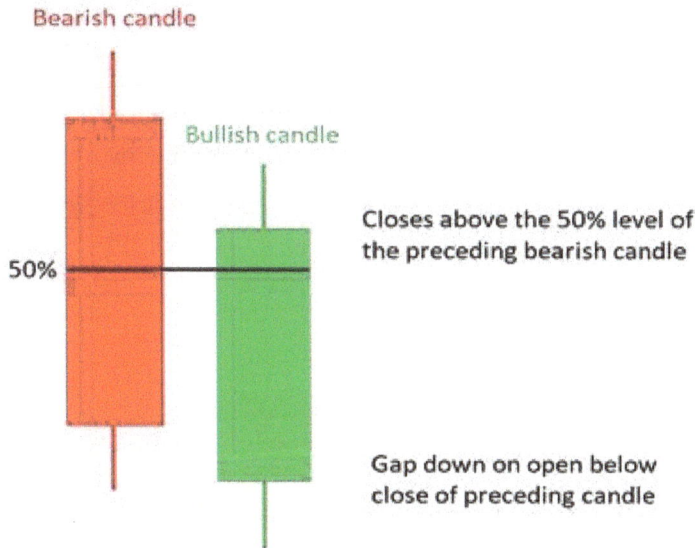

A piercing line candlestick pattern appears during a bullish reversal. It stays at the bottom of a downward trend and it usually causes a reversal trend due to the entrance of the bulls into the market which results in an increase in prices.

The piercing line pattern is characterized by a pair of candlesticks with the proceeding candlestick opening lower than the previous bearish candle. After this, buyers push prices up, causing it to close at above 50% of the bearish candle's body.

This candlestick gets its name from the second day's candle which closes higher than the midpoint of the previous day's candle so it pierces the midpoint of the black candle.

A piercing line candlestick pattern is a two day chart where the first candlestick is substantially influenced by sellers. The second trading day is marked by responses from eager buyers. This is a possible pointer to the fact that the supply features up for sale have become somewhat scarce, and prices have declined to a point where the increase in demand has become very evident.

Forex traders, for example, can trade with the bullish piercing line candlestick pattern when they go long on the second day after the currency gathers momentum, past the middle point of a black day.

Just as it is with every other bullish reversal pattern, you have to look out for extra confirmation. This is because this pattern is only moderately reliable, unlike others that are highly reliable.

In the same light, a trader who has so much to lose would seek more signals pointing at upward reversals in an entire downtrend. This is usually done by looking out for the long white candlestick day. Once this is initiated, the trader can then establish a long position in the market.

What Does the Piercing Line Candlestick Say?

When the piercing line pattern occurs, technical analysts take it as a possible indication of a bullish reversal. The truth is that this pattern is typically rare, but it seems to do better when the downtrend before it stays longer. When a bullish divergence appears at the time when the piercing line candles appear, it boosts its (piercing line's) possibility of being meaningful.

The white candlestick from the second day bounces back from a lower gap to the middle point, then closes high. This should be taken as an indication of attaining the support line. This usually happens because stakeholders in the market set the opening at a price lower than that of the preceding day. As a result, eager buyers come in and cause a reversal from the start of the trading day.

You may, however, confirm this pattern by finding out whether or not it appeared on the support trendline where buying had formerly taken place. The piercing line pattern is usually the only possible pointer towards a reversal so when traders follow the lead of this pattern, they usually look out for breakaway gaps.

Morning Star Candlestick Pattern

Morning Star

The bullish morning star candlestick pattern is a bottom reversal pattern that alerts traders of weak downtrends that might eventually culminate in a trend reversal. Just as it is with the evening star, the morning star is characterized by three candlesticks where the middle candlestick takes the shape of a star. The first candlestick in this pattern is typically a dark candlestick with a large body, while the second candle is the star which is characterized by a short body that stands away from the body of the first candle.

The morning star is not to be mistaken for the doji or spinning top candlestick. The star in the morning star candlestick pattern does not appear under the low of the initial candlestick as it can stay within the initial candle's lower body. The Star is usually the first sign of a weakness as it suggests that sellers failed to push the close price lower than that of the previous day. The role of the third candlestick is to confirm this weakness. This third candlestick has a light color and its close eats into the initial candlestick's body.

What Does the Morning Star Candlestick Say?

This pattern is more of a visual pattern, so it doesn't entail many calculations. It either forms after three trading sessions or not. There are some other variables that can be used to confirm whether the morning star will form. Such variables are whether the price action is close to a support line, or whether the RSI (Relative Strength Indicator) reflects oversold security.

Note that the middle candle in a morning star may either be black, white, red or green when buyers and sellers begin to edge out during a trading session.

Three White Soldiers Pattern

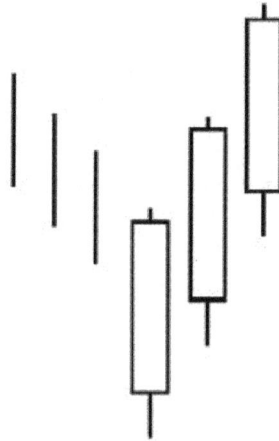

This is another bullish pattern that appears at the base of a downtrend. Just as the name implies, the pattern is made up of three white or green candlesticks. When these candlesticks appear, traders anticipate a future price reversal as a result of strong buying pressure. The three black crows' pattern is the opposite of the three white soldiers.

When you see three green or white candles in a sequence on a chart, it is the three white soldiers' pattern. Each of these candles must open and close in a progressive manner, at a higher rate than the first. The candlesticks are characterized by big bodies and small or without wicks. The pattern is never elsewhere asides from the bottom of a downtrend.

What Do the Three White Soldiers Say?

The three white soldiers indicate that there is a solid change in market sentiment as regards securities which reflects in the price action on the chart. Typically, candles that close with meagre or no shadows imply that the bulls were able to hold the price to the top during a particular session.

This pattern means that the bulls have taken over the rally-all session which closed around the high of the day for three sessions in a row. Also, this pattern may come after other reversal patterns like the doji.

It is possible for a security to remain in a downtrend for many weeks before the bullish reversal takes over. This pattern indicates that the reversal may sustain, but traders are to check other important factors before they decide on whether to buy or sell.

Chapter 7: Bearish Candlestick Reversal Patterns

In the last chapter, we discussed profitable bullish candlesticks patterns, in this chapter, we will be looking at how to use the bearish reversal patterns in candlestick charting.

The bearish reversal candlestick patterns form with either one or more bullish candlesticks. The reversal signifies that the buying pressure is overwhelmed by the selling pressure for a day or more days. However, it is not clear if the sustained selling or the shortage of buyers will keep pushing prices lower. If there is no confirmation, many of the patterns would be seen as neutral and will just be an indicator of a potential resistance level. A bearish confirmation suggests a further downside coming, such as a high-volume decline, gap down, or a long black candlestick. Since candlestick patterns are usually short-term and very efficient for about 1 to 2 weeks, bearish confirmation should be between 1 to 3 days.

For a candlestick pattern to be considered as a bearish reversal, an existing uptrend to reverse should be in existence. This mustn't be a major uptrend, but at least, it should be up for a few days. Bearish reversal patterns in a downtrend suggest an existing selling pressure and should be referred to as continuation patterns.

Candlestick patterns give insights into a price action by just looking. There are basic candlestick patterns that give an insight into what the market is thinking, but sometimes, they may not give accurate signals since they are very common. However, advanced candlestick patterns offer higher reliability. Hence the need to know both.

There are so many types of bearish reversal patterns and below, we'll be looking at some of the basic and advanced bearish candlestick reversal patterns and how to trade with them.

Bearish Engulfing Pattern (Basic)

This pattern shows similarities with the outside reversal chart pattern. However, it doesn't need the entire range, which is low and high, before being engulfed; what it requires is just open and close.

The bearish engulfing candlestick pattern consists of two candlesticks. The first one is white while the second is black. The size of the first isn't important but it shouldn't be a Doji (very easy to engulf). On the other hand, the second one should be a long black candlestick. The bigger the size, the more bearish the reversal is. The first should completely engulf the body of the second. Although it is not a requirement, the black body should also engulf the shadows. It is permitted to engulf shadows, but they are usually nonexistent on both of the candlesticks.

Subsequently, after an advance, the black candlestick will start forming as a result of the security opening above the precious close due to buying pressure. Sellers will then come into the picture after the opening gap, and therefore prices begin to drive down. Selling will be so intense making prices move below the previous open, at the end of the session. The developed candlestick engulfs the previous day's body, creating a possible short-term reversal. More weakness is expected for bearish confirmation of this pattern.

Dark Cloud Cover Pattern (Basic)

This pattern consists of two candlesticks. The first one is white, while the second is black. The two candlesticks have large bodies with small shadows that are usually nonexistent, although this may not always be the case.

The second candlesticks open above the previous close and closes below the middle of the body of the first candlestick. A reversal can be close above the midpoint; however, it may not be bearish.

Similar to the bearish engulfing pattern, there is a forced high price on the open coming from residual buying pressure. This will form an open gap above the body of the white candlestick. Sellers will then come into the picture to push the prices lower after the strong open. The force in selling will then drive prices below the middle of the body of the white candlestick. There will be a further weakness for the bearish confirmation of the dark cloud cover.

Island Reversal Pattern (Advanced)

This is a strong short-term trend reversal signal that is spotted by a gap between a reversal candlestick, with two candlesticks on any of its sides. In the entry, the island reversal pattern indicates indecision alongside a battle between bears and bulls. It is usually indicated by a long-ended Doji candlestick with a high-volume taking place subsequently after an extended trend. A trade is taken after the gap and moves in the opposite direction.

In an exit, you would want to seize the thrust in price following the pattern, but once you notice that the thrust is weakening, then that is your clue to get out. However, if you notice a movement in the price back up to fill the gap, it indicates that the reversal pattern is invalidated, and exiting immediately should be your next move. You can place a stop-loss near the island candlestick or in the gap.

Bearish Harami Pattern (Basic)

This pattern consists of two candlesticks; the first with a large body while the second has a small body that is covered by the first. This pattern has four possible combinations which are white/black, white/white, black/black, and black/white. All Harami look the same, regardless of whether they are bullish or bearish. The preceding trend is what determines their bearish or bullish nature. If there is a decline, Harami is considered a potential bullish reversal, but with an advance, it is considered as a potential bearish reversal. Irrespective of the colour of the first candlestick, as the body of the second candlestick gets smaller, the more likely a reversal. For instance, if the small candlestick is Doji, then there is an increase in the chances of a reversal.

Author and speaker Steve Nison, who is known for pioneering candlestick charts to the western world asserted in his book *Beyond Candlesticks* that any mix of colors can form a Harami, however, the ones that form with a black/black or black/white are the most bearish. Since the first candlestick is characterized by a large body, it indicates that there would be a stronger bearish reversal pattern if it's a black body. As an indication, there would be a rushed and continued increase in the selling pressure. The small candlestick will then signify consolidation before continuation. A potential reversal can still come from the white/black or white/white combination and therefore be considered as a Bearish Harami. The first white candle is formed in the trend's direction, indicating that a significant buying pressure will ensue, however it could also mean that there is excessive bullishness. Subsequently, the small candlestick forms with a gap on the open, signifying a rapid shift in the sellers' direction and a potential reversal.

Kicker Pattern (Advanced)

This is an extraordinarily strong and one of the most reliable candlestick patterns. It is indicated by a sharp reversal in price during the time of the two candlesticks.

For the entry, the price action will inform you that a group of traders has outshined the other, making room for a new trend. Basically, you need to watch out for the gap between the first and second candlesticks, together with high volume. You should enter the kicker candle's close or near the second candles' open.

For the exit, you should place a stop-loss below the kicker candle's low since it can be so large. Your stop-loss should be at a reasonable distance away from your entry point. For a target, the kicker pattern usually results in a strong trend challenge, meaning traders can take advantage of the pattern for a short-term trade, or perhaps a medium-term trade since the price can continue in that direction for a while.

Shooting Star Pattern (Basic)

This pattern consists of one candlestick which is usually black or white, a long upper shadow, a small body, and either a small or non-existent lower shadow. The upper shadow's size should at least double the body's length, and the low/high range should be moderately large.

To have a candlestick in a star position, it should have a gap away from the former candlestick. Greg Morris explained in his book *Candlestick Charting* that a shooting star needs to gap up from the previous candlestick. While Steve Nison in *Beyond Candlesticks* gives an example of a shooting star, forming below the previous close. Opportunity for maneuver should be available, especially when with stocks and indices, it usually opens near the previous close. The robustness of the shooting start is enhanced with a gap up, however, ensure you do not rush the essence of the reversal without the gap.

Hook Reversal Pattern (Advanced)

This is a short- to medium-term reversal pattern that is recognized by a lower high and higher low when compared with the previous day.

Bearish hook reversal pattern

For the entry on the bearish pattern, there is usually an uptrend that is followed by two down days. One of the days will break the low of the last up day. The trade should be taken on the second down day since the pattern will show that the price could go lower. On the bullish side, it is vice versa. There is a downtrend that is followed by two up days. One of the up days will break the high of the last down day. Ensure you take the trade on the second up day as the pattern is showing that price is on the rise.

If you want to trade with this pattern, then you ought to know your exit point first. In many instances, you will notice a sharp reversal. If you notice something else that is contrary to the sharp reversal, then you need to take a U-turn and exit immediately. A stop-loss should then be placed below the recent low for the bullish pattern or above the recent high for a bearish pattern. With just the pattern, we can't be sure of how long the reversal should last. However, you should make sure you maintain the trade if the price keeps moving in the expected direction. Profit should be taken immediately if a pattern in the opposite direction is occurring, or the move weakens.

Evening Star Pattern (Basic)

The evening star consists of three candlesticks: a long white candlestick, a long black candlestick, and a small white or black candlestick. The small white or black candlestick can also be a Doji (an evening Doji star) as it gaps above the body of the previous candlestick. The long white candlestick signifies that buying pressure is strong with the trend remaining high.

As the second candlestick gaps up, there is an additional indication of residual buying pressure. When a small candlestick or gap forms, the advance will slow down greatly or ceases, showing a possible reversal of a trend. The chances of reversal will automatically increase if the small candlestick is a Doji. The long black candlestick gives a bearish confirmation of the reversal.

Bearish Abandoned Baby Pattern (Basic)

This pattern shares so much similarity with the evening Doji star. It consists of three candlesticks which ate a long black candlestick gaping below the low of the Doji, a long white candlestick, and a Doji gapping above the high of the previous candlestick.

The notable differences between these two patterns (bearish abandoned baby and the evening Doji star) are the gaps on either side of the Doji. The first gap indicates an uptrend continuation and a strong buying pressure. Once the gap up and security closes near or exactly at the open, the buying pressure will start subsiding and thus create a Doji. Following the Doji, the long black candlestick and the gap down will hint at a strong selling pressure to bring the reversal to completion. However, more bearish confirmation is needed.

San-Ku (Three Gaps) Pattern (Advanced)

This is an anticipatory trend reversal signal that does not show a precise point of reversal. Instead of showing an exact point, it shows that a reversal may occur in the future. The San-Ku is created by three trading sessions following themselves with gaps in between. Even though each candlestick must not be large, at least two or three of the candlesticks are large. As the price is moving higher, and with the three gaps in a row, the momentum will not be endless; the buyers will get exhausted, and the price will take another direction.

For the entry, the San-Ku runs on the idea that the price may retreat following a sharp move since traders will be taking profits. If you need more evidence for a reversal possibility, then you should seek extremes in the Relative Strength Index (RSI) or wait for a crossover of the Moving Average Convergence Divergence (MACD).

For the exit, you should know that the pattern already expects a reversal, and if it doesn't work that way or doesn't happen, then you need to quit any trade that was taken due to the pattern. For the signal to be valid, the price must go in the expected direction. You can place the stop-loss orders above the high of the pattern if there is an indication that it is going short. You should take advantage of the downward momentum while it lasts. Since the duration of the sell-off is not certain, you should take profits when the selling momentum is slowing down or when you see a reversal signal in the opposite direction.

That is it for both the basic and advanced bearish reversal candlestick patterns. What next?

Have you ever wondered if a decline in a stock price you are holding is short-term or long-term, or even just a market glitch? Does this sound familiar to you? I know many of us have been in this kind of situation, only for us to start seeing the stock price rise, just days after selling off. This is a quite common scenario that can be very frustrating. Even if you can't totally avoid this kind of situation, knowing how to identify and trade retracements will improve your overall performance.

Now, we will be looking at retracement and reversal, and how to spot their differences.

Retracement And Reversal

A reversal is when there is a change in the direction in the price trend of an asset. What this suggests is that the price may likely continue in the direction for a long period. The directional changes may happen to the downside after an upward trend, and to the upside after a downward trend.

The change is usually a huge shift in price. Although pullbacks may take place where the price recovers the previous direction, it is impossible to predict immediately if the price correction is either a continuation of the reversal or a pullback. This change can take days, weeks, years, and even just a sudden shift to materialize.

How to identify reversals:

Retracements on the other hand are temporary price reversals that occur in a larger trend. The prices in retracements are just temporary and don't indicate that there is a change in the larger trend.

Even with retracements, a long-term trend will remain; the stock price may still be going up. Even when the price moves up, there is a new high, and when there is a price drop, it will start rallying before reaching the previous low. This particular movement is a tenet of an uptrend (where there are higher lows and higher highs). If this is happening, then the trend is up. An uptrend makes a lower high and lowers low just once before the trend is drawn into question and a possibility of a reversal forming.

How to identify retracements:

It is crucial for us to know how to differentiate reversal from retracement and that's what we'll be doing in this section. Reverse and retracement have several differences and we need to consider the differences during the classification of a price movement.

While you look at the table below, I want you to remember that when reported, short interest is delayed, so it might be impossible to be certain, depending on your time frame.

Factor	Retracement	Reversal
Chart Patterns	There are just a few, and if any it is reversal patterns that ate limited to candles	Many reversal patterns that usually chart patterns (double top)
Volume	Profit-taking is by retail traders (small block trades)	There is institutional selling (large block trades)
Recent Activity	It usually takes place after large gains	It can occur at any time, even during a regular trading
Short Interest	There is no change in short interest	There is a rising short interest
Money Flow	During a decline, there is a buying interest	There is little buying interest
Candlesticks	"Indecision" candles which usually have long bottoms and tops (spinning tops)	Reversal candles which are usually soldiers, engulfing and other similar patterns
Time Frame	There is a short-term reversal that lasts for not more than one or two weeks	There is a long-term reversal that lasts for weeks
Fundamentals	There is no change in fundamentals	There is usually change or rumor of change in fundamentals

As a calculative trader, you need to learn to differentiate between reversals and retracements because without knowing them, you may miss opportunities, you get to exit sooner than you should, wasting your money on spreads/commissions, holding on to the losing position, and losing money. However, if you combine technical analysis with the measures of basic identification, you can then safeguard yourself from the potential risks, and use your trading capital wisely.

Finally, the bearish reversal candlestick patterns are associated with gaps and strong price moves which usually allow a sharp shift in direction. However, you can participate in it by identifying the patterns and then act quickly to get in while the price is moving in the new direction. There is no price target for candlestick patterns, however, you shouldn't get greedy with it. You should make sure to ride the momentum for the period it lasts for, but when you see signs of trouble, get out of it. Make sure you use trailing stop-loss or stop-loss orders.

Chapter 8: Technical Analysis Price Patterns

As a technical analyst, you might have come across some strange shapes and outlines on trading charts. If you are not very schooled in this area, you may think it's awkward for such uncoordinated patterns and shapes to have any meaning at all. The truth, however, is that these shapes and patterns that are birthed by market price actions will continue to occur if certain interactions take place in the market.

Price patterns indicate market situations that involve statistical edges that traders could exploit so even though they cannot be taken as complete proof, they give traders an edge which they can take advantage of for a long time. This is how the successful day traders you know can make money and stay ahead of others in the market.

To give it a definition, price patterns can be said to be an identifiable set up of price direction which can be identified with the help of curves and/or trendlines. When the price pattern shows that there is a change in the direction of trends, we call it a reversal pattern. There is the continuation pattern which is birthed by a sustained trend based on an already established direction after a short pause. Technical analysts have used price patterns to gain insights into current market trends as well as future trends.

Price patterns at their finest, are formations that help to forecast the mindset of day traders at different price levels. If you can identify the different price patterns, you automatically have an edge over other traders that depend on fundamentals and other technical indicators. Think about it this way, what about being able to accurately point out trade entry points every time currency pairs break out or being able to forecast the extent to which a currency pair will move as soon as it breaks out and starts to move. This is exactly what price patterns arm you with.

Now take a look at the different price patterns and how they are useful to you as a trader.

Continuation Patterns

At some times during a particular trend, the most predominant movement pauses for so many reasons. One of such reasons is that as the trend continues, long buyers will begin to sell with the mindset of making a profit. With this, there is bound to be buying pressure which causes the price to drop.

A synth of this selling and buying pressure leads to sideways price action. Contrarily, a chunk of downward movement sparks short selling to take over, thereby causing buying pressure to counter the downtrend. Note that market trends happen all the time in all markets to create recurrent patterns on charts.

This pattern can, therefore, be defined as a pause in the middle of a predominant trend when the bulls gather momentum in an uptrend or when the bears catch their breath for a while amid a downtrend. As a price pattern forms, traders can't possibly tell whether this is going to be a continuation or reversal so they must pay keen attention to the trendlines. This is to understand the price pattern to know if the price falls below or above the continuation line. The best practice that has worked for me so far is to assume that the trend is going to continue until a reversal is confirmed.

Generally, when a price pattern takes longer to form, the price movement within such a pattern will also take a long time to take shape, the movement is bound to be a significant one once the price breaks either below or above the continuation zone.

Pennants Pattern

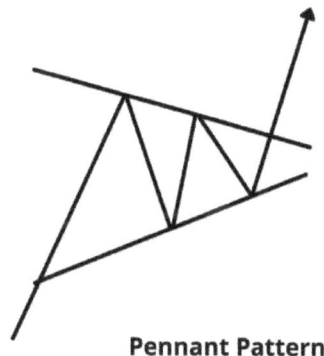

Pennant Pattern

A pennant pattern is typically forecasted by a sudden price rise. It is an almost vertical rise in prices that is also known as the flagpole or the mast. The two trend lines that come together to form the pennants pattern are down trend lines which stand for the no-so-highs. They can also be upward trend lines that stand for the lesser lows.

A pennant pattern that forms after a sharp downward move tends to keep sliding downwards and can be seen as a bearish pennant, while the pennant that forms after a sharp upward trend will be taken as a bullish pennant.

It is important to note that pennants usually appear around midway through the whole price movement so any move that follows the breakout of the pennant will carry the same weight as the flagpole.

Flag Pattern

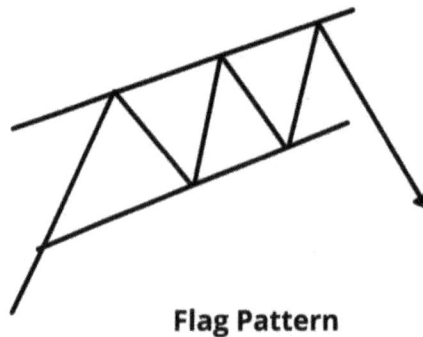

Flag Pattern

Flags come to life after two parallel slopy parallel trend lines come together in either an upward, downward or sideways/horizontal movement. Generally, when a flag is in an upward slope, it shows as a pause in a market downtrend. This means that a flag that aligns itself downwards portrays a break in a market uptrend. In most cases, when the flag forms, it is followed by a decline in volume which picks up as soon as the price breaks away from the flag formation.

The flag pattern in a market chart has the shape of a sloping rectangle which has support and resistance lines that are parallel until a breakout happens. The breakout typically comes in the opposite direction of the trendlines. This means that the flag pattern is a reversal pattern.

Wedge Patterns

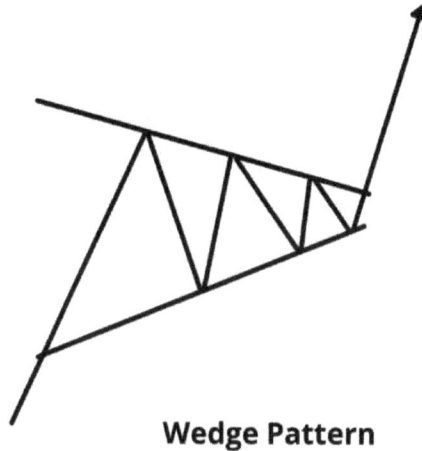

Wedge Pattern

The wedge pattern stands for the tight price movement that stands within the support and resistance lines which may either be a rising or falling wedge. Unlike what is obtainable with the triangle pattern, the wedge pattern does not include a horizontal trend line, but it is either marked by a couple of upward or downward trend lines.

When the wedge is a downward one, it means that there will be a price break in the resistance line. An upward wedge, however, indicates that the price will break from the support line. This, however, proves that the wedge is a reversal pattern because its breakout is in contrast to the general trend.

Triangles

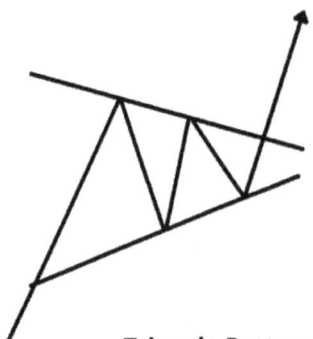

Triangle Pattern

Triangles are some of the most popular price patterns you'll come across in technical analysis because you are likely to come across them more than every other pattern. The most popular triangles are the ascending, symmetrical, and descending triangles. These patterns can stay for as long as weeks to many months.

For triangles like symmetrical triangles, they happen when two trend lines come together facing each other to indicate that a breakout is about to happen. It doesn't show direction. Ascending triangles on the other hand can be identified by their flat up trend line and their rising low trend lines which indicates that a high breakout may happen. The up-trend lines in descending triangles indicate that there might be either breakouts or breakdowns. The weight of either the breakdowns or the breakouts usually stands at the same height as the triangle's left vertical side.

Let's go deeper into understanding the three types of triangles one after the other:

Symmetric Triangles:

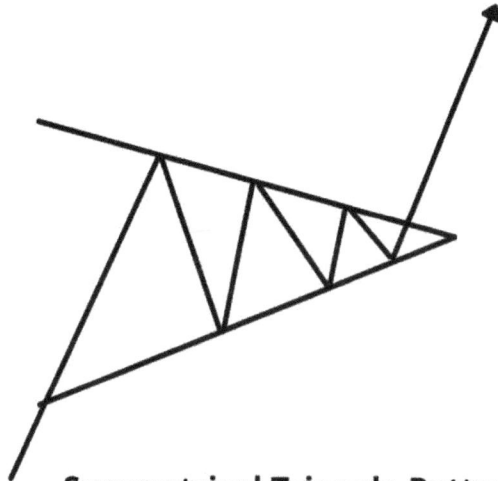

Symmetrical Triangle Pattern

Symmetric triangles come to life following the meeting of the connecting lines of the highs with the trendline that links the lows, such that it forms a triangle. These patterns are marked by a down trendline as well as an up trendline that comes together.

Because the two lines of the ascending triangle are marked by the same slope, it isn't quite possible to predict its direction. In most cases, there is a possibility of a breakout from one direction or the other. One can't tell which direction it will be. The direction of the triangle is also neither upward nor downward and this is because the slope of the two lines reflects one another.

The role of this pattern is to tell traders that the existing trend before the formation of the pattern will continue even after the price breaks away from the triangle.

Ascending Triangle:

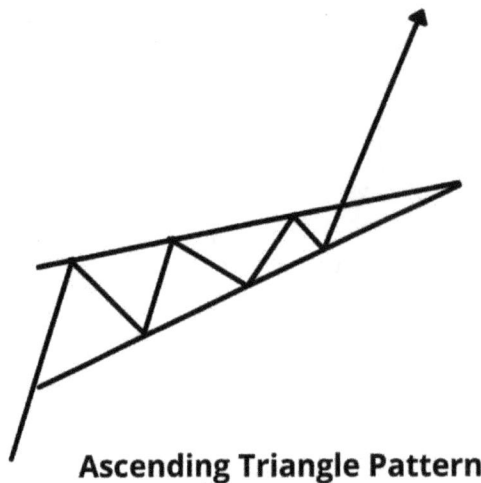

Ascending Triangle Pattern

This pattern is characterized by a flat line that accompanies the highs that remains at almost the same price as well as an up-trend line that follows the higher lows. In a nutshell, this trend indicates that the highs will remain the same while the lows increase.

When this pattern appears, it means that buying pressure is more than the selling pressure which will eventually end in a breakout at the upside.

Descending Triangle:

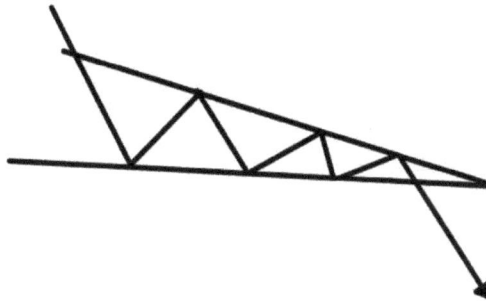

Descending Triangle Pattern

The descending triangle pattern can be likened to an upturned ascending triangle. This means that rather than facing up, it faces down.

This pattern is birthed by a flat slope at the base of the trendline as well as a sharp downward slope above the trendline. The descending triangle pattern indicates that sellers are taking over from buyers and forcing prices to decline. It is a bearish continuation pattern that forecasts a downward breakdown as soon as the pattern breaks.

Rounding Bottom

The rounding bottom pattern which is also known as the cup forecasts a bullish uptrend. The middle of the U shape presents traders with the opportunity to buy by taking advantage of the bullish trend that comes after the breakthrough from the resistance levels.

Cup and Handles

The cup and handle patterns are immensely popular continuation patterns in day trading and other stock markets. They forecast the coming of a bullish trend. It is like the rounding bottom pattern in a lot of ways, but unlike the rounding bottom, this pattern has a handle after the rounding bottom. The handle looks like a pennant or a flag and once it is completed, traders can easily see market breakouts in bullish uptrends.

This bullish continuation pattern forms when an upward trend pauses to continue after the formation of the pattern is confirmed. The cup part of the pattern forms a 'U' shape that is similar to a round bowl as opposed to the typical 'V' shape which has equal heights on the two ends of the cup.

The 'handle' part of this pattern takes shape on the cup's right side as a short pullback. The expected stock breakout in new highs doesn't happen until the handle is completely formed. It continues to trend higher after it resumes.

Gaps

Gaps are usually formed after a space within two trading periods as a result of a notable boost or decline in prices. A security can, for example, close at $10.00 and open at $12.00 after some earnings or other contributors.

Gaps are categorized into three distinct types which are the runaway, breakaway and exhaustion gaps. While runaway gaps are formed at the middle of a trend, breakaway gaps form at the beginning of the trend. Exhaustion gaps on the other hand form somewhere close to the end of the trend.

Head and Shoulders Pattern

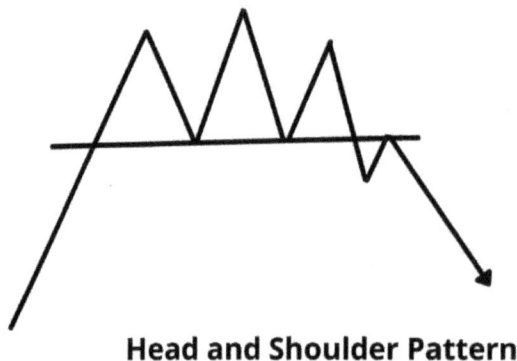

Head and Shoulder Pattern

The head and shoulders pattern forms to forecast the transition from bull to bear market reversal. This pattern is marked by a big peak which has two other small peaks at both sides. The three levels in this pattern drop to the same support level after which it is expected to break out in a downward movement.

This pattern may form at the top or bottom of the market in a series of three different pushes. The first is known as the initial peak or tough, while the second one is the larger one. The third push takes the form of the first one.

When there is an interruption in an uptrend by the head and shoulders pattern, it is most likely followed by a trend reversal which eventually leads to a downtrend. Contrarily, when a downtrend leads to the heads and shoulders bottom, it is likely to culminate in an upward trend reversal.

It is not unusual for horizontal or sloppy trendlines to form, then connect the peaks and the troughs which reflect within both the head and shoulders. There may be a decline in volume as the pattern is formed. The volume, however, springs up as soon as the price breaks above the head and shoulders bottom or below the top of the head and shoulders on the trendline.

Double Bottom

Double Bottom Pattern

This pattern is the reverse of the double top pattern. It takes the shape of the letter 'W' and shows that the price has tried to break through the support level at two different times. This is a reversal chart pattern because it indicates a price reversal. After the two unsuccessful attempts at breaking through the support line, the market moves towards an upward trend.

Double Top

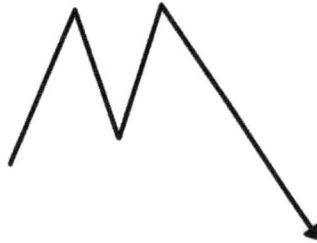

Double Top Pattern

This is the opposite of the double bottom pattern. It takes the shape of the letter 'M' and falls into the reversal trend after two failed attempts at pushing through the resistance level. The trend eventually falls back to the support base, then begins a downward trend which pushes through the support line.

Both the double tops and bottom patterns signal at the points where the market tried to push through the support or resistance level twice without any success. The double top on the other hand is marked by the previous push up to the resistance level which precedes a second failed attempt then culminates in a trend reversal.

Summarily, price patterns form after prices take a pause. They point towards those areas where there may be a consolidation that would either result in a reversal or a continuation of a dominant trend. Trendlines are particularly important aspects of understanding these price patterns as they can appear in different forms like double tops, flags, cups, or pennants.

Volume is also another especially important aspect of this pattern. They usually decline as the pattern forms, then increase when there is a price breakout from the pattern. As a technical analyst, you should be able to use price patterns to predict future price trends which would include both continuations and reversals.

Chapter 9: Using Candlestick Charts To Spot Trends

———— ✺ ————

To carry out technical analysis, prices need to be well represented on a chart. Candlestick charts will give you, as a technical analyst, a visual representation of the market. As you gather enough experience and over time, you can easily analyze the market conditions and make good decisions through technical analysis.

In this chapter, I will be providing you with the knowledge on how you can easily spot trends with candlestick charting. I believe that by the end of this chapter, you should be well equipped with the right information to support you and make good trading decisions when using candlestick charts.

Perhaps, you have heard the adage that says, "*trade with the trend.*" Well, this may not be far from the truth because, according to the trend, all pundits are your friend. This should work for you if you know and accept that trends can end and will not be in your favor, which brings us to the importance of knowing the direction of the trend.

I believe that at this point, you are now familiar with looking at charts and spotting familiar chart patterns (this includes a reversal breakout). If you want to spot a possible breakout, then you need to get accustomed to trend lines and drawing trend lines on a chart.

Trend Lines

Trend lines are a technical analysis tool drawn at an angle either above or below the price. This tool is used to give indications as to when a trend changes and as to the immediate trend. It connects a swing low to a swing high (the lowest point of the down movement and the highest point of the up movement). When a price rises, the trend line will also rise. Consequently, when a price falls, the swing highs also fall. By connecting, the highs with a line will give a descending trend line that shows a downward trend.

Trend lines can also be used as support and resistance, providing opportunities to open and close positions.

Trend lines could be an awesome tool if you used them correctly. If not used right, it will be ineffective. It can even be counterproductive, resulting in wrong beliefs that a trend has strength even when price action suggests that it doesn't or when prices have made a reversal.

Drawing Trend Lines

Trend lines should be drawn above the price when drawing in a downtrend. In an uptrend, it should be drawn below the price. The lows on an uptrend and highs on a downtrend is what determines a trend line. Two or more swing highs are required for a trend line to be drawn in either direction.

For a valid trend line, three or more lows and highs are needed. Basically, the more the price reaches a trend line, the more valid it becomes because many traders use them as support and resistance.

Some traders use the bodies of the candlesticks when drawing trend lines, while others use the wicks. Even though the use of the bodies of the candlestick is the most acceptable way of drawing trend lines on a chart, many traders prefer using the wicks.

Chart below demonstrating a trend line drawn with the wicks of candlesticks.

Chart below showing a trend line drawn with the body of candlesticks.

You can see that both ways from the charts above. Since trend lines are subjective, you should make use of what you are more comfortable with. However, whichever method you choose, ensure you do not deviate.

Trading does not work on luck alone. For you to succeed with trading, you have to cultivate trading skills and learn to enhance them. Your trades should be based on detailed research, reading patterns, charts, analysis, trading trends and indicators. This brings us to trend-following, which is another common strategy that many traders rely on in getting their investment to its fruition.

Trend Following

Do you know that Richard Dennis, who founded the Turtle Traders, made $400 million trading the futures market? In fact, Jesse Livermore, the renowned and most famous trader, made $100 million in 1929? Within 16 years, Ed Seykota, who is possibly the best trader of our time, achieved a return of 250,000%.

That is huge, right? Of course, it is. But what exactly is their trading approach? This brings us to the definition of trend following.

Trend following is a method of trading that captures the various trends happening across different markets. This strategy works on the idea that as traders ride the trend, losses can be avoided. This way, securities are bought before the price goes up, and it is sold before it goes down. As a trend follower, before you invest, you need to properly implement risk management strategies. You don't aim to forecast or predict a trend. You just follow the existing trend and watch out for emerging trends in the market.

You may be wondering why trend following work. The reason is simple. As we all know, markets are driven by emotions such as fear, emotions, and greed. According to the words of popular trader Jesse Livermore, *"I believe that price movement patterns are being repeated. They are recurring patterns that appear over and over, with slight variations. This is because markets are driven by humans, and human nature never changes."* Therefore, when a side is in charge, a trend emerges while the trend followers take advantage of the trend.

How Trend Followers Make Money

As a trend follower, you are reducing errors and focusing more on technical analysis and data. It is less risky and makes you focus more on trends within different industries and stocks. If you are patient enough and willing to wait, then it can be a good way to trade.

So, how do trend followers make money?

Let's imagine this scenario. For over 6 months, a company called Kreative Kubes has been trading higher. Currently, Kreative Kubes trades at $200, and it's seen as overvalued. You then decide to short 2000 shares of Kreative Kubes at $200 with a profit target of $180, using the no stop loss. If you apply this technique across all the markets, you are trading (a small profit target without stop loss), what then will happen? You will win many times. However, there will be a trade that will go against you until you blow up your trading account.

But what if you are on the opposite side of the trade?

You will lose many times too, but it requires just trade to make it all back, and even more. Remembering that the same trade caused your account to blow up.

A real-life example is the 2008 financial crisis and the fall of long-term capital management, where traders and investors lost tons of money. However, in a zero-sum game, while someone is losing, someone is winning. In this case, the winners are the trend followers.

Strategies For Trend Following

Why traders devise a strategy for trading with trend following is to profitably take advantage of the various market scenarios. The market is a high-risk, high-reward market, as you already know. A general perception is often created based on the opinions of the market influencers or leaders, and soon enough, there will be a buzz that makes investors interested. The technical analysis of market data gives birth to this buzz, while the other significant aspects that relate to trading are measured too. This way, traders will then try to identify various parameters that govern trade, and then trend following strategy will fall into place. Note, you should not rely on just an indicator to predict how you should buy and sell stocks securely. Typically, you need to combine different strategies to form a trend-following trading system. Strategies for trend following are:

Head and Shoulders: This is a popular trend-following strategy or indicator that is used by many traders. The head and shoulders strategy indicates when a trend reaches its end and when a new trend is emerging. This strategy can also work upside down. The head will represent the lowest or highest price reached by security, while the shoulder represents the two low or two high points.

Bollinger Bands: This is a helpful trend following indicator that assumes there will be a comeback of the price of securities. The Bollinger band measures volatility and reveals the lowest and highest points of security. It can be used in ranging markets, uptrend, and downtrends.

Moving Averages: This strategy will signify an underlying trend behind security. Moving averages are of different types, but trend followers use the slow-moving average more. This will help them focus on the original price and direction of the trend. Also, it will hinder temporary changes in trend prices.

Trend Following Principles You Should Follow

- You may not have a certain profit target as a trend follower but lacking a certain target does not mean you should also not set a stop/loss target.

- Ensure you buy securities at a high price and sell at a higher price.

- Make use of a proper risk management strategy and not risk more than just a fraction of your trade capital.

- Enter into trades in various markets, rather than just limit your trade to one market place. By doing this, you are increasing your chances of recognizing and following different trends.

- Since market predictions can cloud your judgment, avoid making them. Try following the price instead of losing objectivity and making dangerous trading mistakes.

Finally, trend lines help signify short-term trends in the general trend. Ensure you pay close attention to price action and put it into consideration when using trend lines. It's still a downtrend if the price makes lower lows and lower highs, regardless of the price moving above a descending trend line. It's an uptrend if the price makes higher highs and higher lows, even if it moves below the trend line.

It's important for trend lines to be adjusted often, especially if it is day trading. If you want to avoid constant adjusting, then you should use trend lines "best fit." These will show the trend and when it's reversing and alert you of potential trade opportunities.

Using Candlestick Charts to Recognize False Breakouts

Most times, breakout trading can be rewarding, especially in volatile markets. However, it is often plagued with false breakout and signals, which can be discouraging to even experienced traders.

False breakouts are easily the pet peeves of novice day traders. Forex, stock, or futures may be looking set to move one direction after a breakout, and suddenly, false breakouts jump in, and the price will quickly revert course and put you in a losing direction. This can be very frustrating, but that should not be the case. You need to switch your mind frame from being the victim to being the opportunist.

In this section, we will be looking at what false breakouts are and how you can avoid them.

What Exactly Are False Breakouts?

False breakouts are just how they sound. They are a breakout that has failed to move past a level and results in a false breakout of the level. One of the crucial price action trading patterns you should learn is false breakout patterns. It is often a strong clue that the direction of a price is changing or that a trend will soon resume.

A false breakout can be seen as 'trickery' by the market. It will make it look like there will be a breakout of the price, and then it quickly reverses. As a result, traders that took the bait will all get deceived.

Most times, amateurs enter a market that looks like an 'obvious' breakout, and the professionals will be at the other way pushing the market back. As a smart price action trader, you would want to use false breakouts to your advantage and not fall for them.

Note, false breakouts can be in different forms. Sometimes, it occurs with a "fakey" pattern, with a pin bar pattern, and sometimes, it doesn't.

Examples of of a chart with false breakouts above and below key levels:

Let's look at how you can use false breakouts to your advantage.

Regardless of the source of a breakout, whether from a range or another chart pattern, the idea behind a breakout strategy is to seize a big move after an easy to spot pattern.

If you trade breakouts, it can work. However, you should be ready to experience more false breakouts; the price will break out of the pattern and then return in. If you constantly experience false breakouts, then the market is trying to tell you something. So, instead of trading the breakout, why not trade the false breakout? If you are losing money as a result of false breakouts, then you could make some money together with other traders that are taking it. Although, this strategy requires focus, practice, and quick reflexes.

How To Avoid A False Breakout With Candlestick Charts

This is amazingly simple! As I have suggested above, instead of acting on trade in real-time after noticing price breaks at a key level, you should rather wait for the candle to close to ensure the strength of the breakout.

Some traders set entry orders below or above support or resistance levels to get them into a breakout trade automatically. The truth is this idea is not very smart. Entry orders can make traders get "wicked" into breakout trades that will not materialize. This can even lead us to believe that being at trading terminals and set to act as the candle closes in breakout territory is the only way to trade breakouts effectively. As soon as the candle closes, the trader's position can be opened, and perhaps, have a high chance of success. But what happens in the case when you can't sit all day and expect a breakout?

You can use a price alert that uses the closing price of each candle as its trigger. That is, you only get an alert when the support or resistance is broken and remains broken through the particular candle's close. This way, you will receive an alert, then you can log in and place the trade. The feature of price alert is free in most of the trading platforms in the world.

After selection, you will only get an alert if a candle closes beyond the selected price level instead of getting an alert when the price is broken in real-time. In the case of an hourly chart, you can only get an alert at the top of the hour following the close of each bar, and this is what we want. This little tweak can greatly impact your breakout trading. If you can, make the changes to your strategy with a demo before testing them with real money.

Finally, a candlestick chart can be an important tool for traders that seek a long-term investment opportunity. Overall, traders can use candlestick charts to indicate the time to enter and exit a trade.

Chapter 10: Top Secrets- Why Candlestick Patterns Work

As a trader, you always have to remember that candlestick patterns cannot drive markets on their own. These patterns are not a yardstick or a template with which you can outrightly make market decisions without other variables of technical analysis like the support and resistance level.

That said, you should also beware of the fact that candlesticks work just as they are expected to. A candlestick pattern chart analyzes the market for a certain period and presents you with a summary. Your interpretation of the summary now determines the result you'll get from it. In every chart, the OHLC is very important, such that by blending it with other features like the color of the candle, you can easily tell whether or not the market value appreciated or depreciated during the open or close.

These are the two major things that the candlestick shows you at a particular time;

1. The range of prices that are obtainable for the period under review.

2. The price movement during the said period.

When I said the candlestick chart works as best as it should, this is what I meant. Now try not to let your emotions or imagination push you to want to force the chart to do more than this. It is as a result of such desires that you'll hear people saying that candlestick charts don't work.

The only way you can clearly interpret what a candlestick pattern is trying to tell you is by knowing how to read it. With this knowledge, you could easily tell what the pertinent market dynamics are, as well as the market trend. You will also be able to tell whether or not buyers and sellers control the market at a particular time.

If as a trader you can follow price trends to interpret the psychology of major players in the market, you will be able to apply this knowledge to reading your charts and seizing every opportunity once you see one.

It isn't uncommon to find traders who do not believe in the efficacy of candlesticks. A quick look at trading platforms will show you that there are a lot of trading techniques that use candlestick patterns to trade. Since these patterns are now applied to many trading strategies, it simply means that it works and it holds some sort of market advantage. The reason why it isn't working for you is only because of your unrealistic, albeit uninformed expectations.

There is certainly no way to find out which percentage of traders have candlestick charts working for them because, of a truth, I haven't carried out any of such survey yet, but if this pattern works for as much as 50% of traders, it means that you can find out which patterns hold the most potential for you. You should be able to make a good amount of profit by interpreting these patterns correctly, else you lose money.

These patterns already work for many traders and technical analysts, including myself because we are able to marry the patterns with other technical indicators like the support and resistance level to give us the information we need. A candlestick pattern that is devoid of the support or resistance lines will not work as well as one that has the lines running through.

A trader that knows how to interpret his candlesticks correctly can understand the information presented by the chart about market dynamics and psychology. Such traders will also know the predominant traits in traders at a particular time.

When a trader can trail the path of the price action and can give the right interpretation to the psychology of other market players, he will make a lot of profit. This profit will come from his/her expertise in blending knowledge with price action to read charts and make the best decisions.

Top Candlestick Secrets

To one who is just getting started with technical analysis, candlestick charting may seem too complicated, but it's only normal. With time, as you continue to read and analyze charts, you'll get a hang of it as the patterns will become more familiar by the day. You will also get to learn about the possibility of combining patterns to figure out the current state of the market and to get insights into future trends. You will also learn how to recognize patterns.

As you work towards becoming a professional technical analyst and a profit yielding trader, you need to start thinking in a smart way and learn how to avoid common mistakes, especially beginner mistakes. Remember that your goal with the candlestick chart is to know how buyers and sellers influence price, and to know who is in control of the market at a particular time.

Asides from knowing what a candlestick pattern presents to you, some other concepts will help you to spot high probability price action signals and to avoid those signals that are very likely to lead to a dead end. In trading price action, you need to be very thorough as you make sure that you don't just hop on any signal that you see. To be a successful trader, you need to be flexible by understanding that there are no fixed rules in trading. Below are two important concepts that can lead you to a very successful trading journey:

Comparison of candles: this area of trading when it comes to price action is often ignored because traders are used to focusing on the basic pattern which makes them concern themselves with single candlesticks.

Traders that want to be successful in trading price action must know how to set their recent prices based on the events of the past. Understand that a small pinbar, for example, which appears after a trend with big candles will have less meaning than a large pinbar that shows after a trend with small candles. Another example is an engulfing candle that doesn't fully engulf the preceding one. Such candles don't have as much predictive power as the one that fully engulfs the previous one. You should learn to study the entire chart to fully understand all the variables.

Location: This is another concept that can help you get the best out of your candlestick chart. It simply means that the only time you trade price action signals that are close to high probability price levels. You do not have to hop on every price action signal that comes your way, rather, you can boost your odds and make them work in your favour by setting your trade close to high impact support and resistance levels or the demand and supply levels. Even though trading requires more patience, you will reap the benefits of your patience tremendously.

Candlesticks Trading Secrets 101

Traders are faced with making different market decisions every day, due to the range of factors that influence the market. This is where candlesticks trading patterns come into play as they help you navigate a variety of options that the market bombards you with every trading day. Remember, market players take actions based on emotions like the fear of losses, the hope of gaining, stop-loss triggers, etc. the role of candlestick charts is to help you make informed decisions regardless of these emotions.

By learning how to trade with candlestick patterns, you would have armed yourself with a solid weapon for profitability. Every candle has a unique insight for the trader who can read and interpret the current state of price actions correctly. Once you are able to decipher the information about the market on the candlestick chart, you will have an edge over every other trader.

At this point, you might be wondering how you can trade with the long list of candlestick patterns and how they can give you the desired result. In fact, you even wonder how it is possible to remember all the candlestick patterns. Well, the truth is that you don't have to remember all the patterns. There are two important factors that you need to understand to get you started with analyzing your candlestick chart for the best results. First, you should always ask yourself, where is the close price in relation to the range? The second question is, what is the size of a pattern compared to other candlestick patterns?

Let me give answer and context to these questions.

1. Where is the close price in relation to the range? This question is important to help you know those that are in control at the moment. When for example, the price closes around the highs of the range, it means that the buyers are in control at that time. There are contrary scenarios where bullish candles have sellers in control. This happens when the price closes around the lows of the range indicating that there is a rejection of high prices. What matters most is that you always know who is in control by asking the simple question, "where is the close price in relation to the range?"

2. What is the size of a pattern compared to other candlestick patterns? The answer to this question will help you understand if the price movement is a strong or weak one. To get the answer that you seek, simply compare the size of the current candle with that of the previous one. If for example, the current candle is up to two times larger than the previous one, it means that the move is a strong one. The move will be a weak one if there isn't any strength behind the move because the size of the current candle is about the same as the previous ones.

Common Mistakes Traders Should Avoid

It's very easy for anyone to trade, but when it comes to sustaining it, then it becomes tough. Lots of discipline and planning is involved if you want to make profits. It is always important that you trade patiently, slowly, logically, and most of all, avoid making mistakes.

Mistakes are common in the market, especially among novice traders. However, if you are aware of the common mistakes involved in trading, then you can become more efficient with your trade. We can't take away the fact that all traders make mistakes, regardless of their trade experience. What you need is to understand the logic behind the mistakes, and you may be limiting the effect of reducing the effect of trading impediments.

Below, we'll be looking at the common mistakes' traders make and why they should be avoided. Mistakes are always part of your learning process, so you need to familiarize yourself with them to ensure you don't repeat them.

Misusing Instruments (Stop Loss, Indicators, and Candlesticks)

Many people are guilty of this. They tend to misuse the instruments that are meant for a better chance at success with trade, and this may backfire. Ensure you understand the variables and main factors of trading and how they relate to each other before you start using them. I have already given a detailed guide on using stop-loss, indicators, and candlesticks in this book. Ensure you go through the information carefully to get a better edge at your trade, rather than acting blindly.

Having No Plan

If you base your trade on just random trade ideas and gut feelings, you will make a terrible mistake. A plan is needed before action should be taken; even the law of attraction states that. Don't get me wrong, I support having goals together with a positive attitude. However, trading is different, you can't expect something to happen, and it will just happen that way. The market is an uncertain environment where anything can happen (no built-in system to follow).

Your plan should have how you will enter and exit a trade, which is your trading strategy, and also how to cope with the psychological pressures that come with it.

Giving Huge Capital to A Single Trade

Losses are part of trading. When using some strategies, over 50% of your trade may incur losses. However, you should be able to make up for the losses by having larger profits than losses. You need to be mentally ready if that may be the case. However, you also need to play smart with your capital. Manage your capital well by not allocating too much capital to just a trade. The reason is, you may not know the trade that will do well and those that would not.

Sometimes, it may seem as if you know the direction the trade is going like it is the trade of the moment, and you will become tempted to invest huge funds into that trade. Well, you do have an equal opportunity to make a profit today and tomorrow, so don't tie your money down to a single trade.

Not Paying Attention to Exits

Many people would rather pay more attention to trade entries than trade exits. This should be the case because having a good exit strategy will result in bigger gains or smaller losses; it all depends on the situation. I know how challenging planning an exit strategy can be. However, it is important to dedicate time to tweaking your stop placements or mapping out your exit strategy before your stop gets hit. If your stop is set at a reasonable level and you don't move it from there, then you should be good.

It's always difficult to exit a profitable trade. There will be the desire to quickly take your profits once your position is in green. Even when you set a profit, you will still have doubts, thinking whether there will be a reversal or if you should add to your position. You shouldn't stress yourself about all these because involving emotions would allow you to make irrational decisions. The best thing you can do is to test set-ups as much as you can, then choose the one showing the best result.

Trading With More Than You Can Afford to Lose

Not every day is a rainy day with trading; some days may come with losses (ensure your profit is way more than your losses). It becomes a problem when you trade with more than you can afford to lose. Always make sure you trade with a certain percentage of the amount you can do away within a day. If you know you can cope with a 4% loss, then make sure you discipline yourself to stop there. Stick to your strategy and use only the money you've set aside.

Doing Minimal research

When you study the market as it should be, you get to understand market trends, the fundamental influences, and the timing of entry and exit points. The more dedicated you are to the market, the more understanding of the product you get. Within the market, there are subtle nuances between different pairs and how they work. Therefore, to succeed, you need to thoroughly examine the differences.

Trading Based On Emotions

If you are impatient or emotional when it comes to trading, it will only lead to irrational decisions that result in unsuccessful trades. Smart traders will open up additional positions after losing trades; this will compensate for the lost trades.

Not Practicing With A Demo Account

This is very important. You should never skip the opportunity of getting yourself acquainted with trading with a demo account before entering the real deal. This will also determine the broker's seriousness with its services, giving a risk-free and comprehensive hands-on introduction into trading by offering an educational structure before taking it further with a live trading account with real funds.

Setting Unrealistic Goals

If you are new to the world of trading, you must be patient because you can't make a lot of money in a short time. I know there are exceptions, but there are exceptions everywhere, and there is a slim chance that you will be the next one so fast. If you have this notion, you will likely go down the same road as many traders, which can be tough for you.

Don't get me wrong; I am not saying you can't be successful. In fact, returns will compound over time, even with small capital. Although, many traders do not know what it takes to get to that point. Having successful trading comprises a mix of mindset, knowledge, and personal traits. These are all that you can develop, but you have to involve hard work and commitment. Else, you are plotting to fail. Ensure you set more realistic goals.

Trading Against the Trend

A simple way to achieve success in forex is to trade with the trend. In fact, you get to enjoy the added benefit by trading less, more time and fewer commissions. Even with this, many traders still try to catch market tops and bottoms. I know you can do what works best for you. However, if you keep struggling to see results, then you should reconsider trading trends.

Delaying With Cutting Your Losses

I often wonder why many traders do not like closing losing trades. I see some traders postponing closing trades and hoping for a reversal in a bid to avoid regret in the long run. Many times, this backfires because you will get kicked out of the market either due to one huge loss or a string of losses. Instead of postponing, you should aim to take the loss while it is still small. The loss is already inevitable, so taking risky gambles to avoid that loss can only land you in more trouble as you enter into greater loss.

If you want to keep your account safe and ensure it grows over time, make sure you don't risk more than 1% to 2% of your capital per trade.

Overlooking Long Timeframes

Many traders care less about long timeframes because they are not patient with waiting for trading signals. They prefer to make as many trades as they can in a bid to increase their chances of profit. Unfortunately, it often leads to poor trades, costing you money. If you put quality before quantity, then you should see nothing wrong in trading on smaller charts, especially if you have a working system.

If you are just getting started with trade, then trading longer charts isn't a bad idea. To date, no evidence shows that trading frequently is more profitable. The difference lies in your time commitment and personality. If trading with a system that works on a longer chart is okay with you, then you don't need to trade that much, giving you more time to do other things.

Finally, trading can be very profitable, but it is easy to make mistakes, especially as a beginner. I hope that the common mistakes I've shared with you here will educate you better to spot the things to avoid and what to do better. As a beginner, I would advise that you read and understand this book before going on live trading. If you are experienced, you can still use this book as a guide to ensure you are steering clear of mistakes.

Conclusion

———————— ∽ ————————

It's been an amazing ride from the Introduction, through the ten intense chapters of this book, and it is an absolute delight to have you come this far. I am confident that at this point, you have become ten times a better trader than you were when you started reading this book.

The world has since moved past the analogue and traditional times, and I am glad to have you as one of those who have since realized the need to stay updated in knowledge for the best of the digital world. Day trading, forex, cryptocurrency and many other types of digital trade has since taken over the world to become a force in the financial sector. But as much as these trades have so much to offer to the millennial who wishes to make the most profits from his securities, there're a lot of risks involved. To tell the truth, you can rarely see any trader who hasn't lost some bucks in the past, but that is how you learn to become better and smarter. Perhaps, you have also lost some which isn't a weakness, because I have also- it is a natural part of the path you have chosen to thread.

To give you more insights about the market, and to help you better navigate the market, the Japanese candlestick has proven to be a very handy tool that traders have used across ages. From the times of Sokyu Homma, the Japanese rice trader who is reputed to have studied market patterns and trends, to the present times when traders across the world have embraced this trading technique as a way of studying price movement, the candlestick chart has remained reliable.

By studying the OHLC (Open, High, Low, Close) using different features like the trendlines, moving averages, support and resistance, etc., traders can tell the direction of price movements such that they can make informed decisions rather than depending on their emotions to decide when and how to trade. It is no longer news that traders usually base their market decisions on emotions of fear, hope and anxiety. This may sometimes prove fatal for traders as these emotions may not reflect the real market situation at a particular time. Now, this is why you need a technique that helps you forecast the market future for maximum gains.

The question then becomes, how does one accurately use such a complicated technique as the candlestick chart? If you have read through this book carefully, this question will no longer come from you as you must already know that as much as the candlestick chart looks complicated and technical, you only need a good understanding of the patterns and the way they work to be able to trade seamlessly with it. At what price did the market open? At what price did the market close? Is it the bulls that are in charge of the market at this point? Is it the bears? These are very pertinent questions that the technical analyst asks every trading day to know when to strike and when to lay low and anticipate.

To study the open, high, low, close variables, you have to first understand the different candlestick patterns, which means that you need to also know what candlesticks are first. This is why I took my time to introduce you to the concept of candlestick charting by highlighting the meaning of candlesticks and explaining what you stand to gain from using this charting system. I went ahead to give a precise definition of the candlestick as a method of technical analysis while I also went back in time to discuss how this trading technique came to be. You may have in the past wondered why these patterns usually have just two colors which are either red and green or white and black. Now you know what the colors stand for and why the candles tend to assume such color at a particular point in trading time.

Before introducing you to the different types of candlestick patterns, this book takes a short pause to weigh candlesticks and bar charts against each other, exploring their similarities and differences as well as their advantages and disadvantages. This chapter aims to help you understand why candlesticks tend to continue to grow in popularity against other equally useful charts in the market.

Technical analysis is home which accommodates the various forms of market analysis, but how do we talk about an arm of the house without looking at the entire house to know why the arm under study is the way it is? For a deeper understanding of the intricacies of candlestick charts, you, therefore, need to know a thing or more about technical analysis, from the basics to the major indicators in technical analysis. As you must have learned from experience, risk management is an especially important part of any trading regardless of how small it may be. I, however, trust that by now, you must have learned some risk management strategies that you will carry along with you every step of your trading journey.

This book is an easy guide to understanding the anatomy of candlesticks which is a perfect way for you to read candlestick charts. While there are many types of candlestick patterns that have different names, there are only two determinants for these patterns. They are either bullish or bearish. The simple way to look at it is that the market is bearish when the opening price is higher than the closing price, while it is bullish when the opening price is lower than the closing price. The engulfing or reversal patterns may be either bullish or bearish depending on their opening or closing price.

This book aims at helping you to become an expert technical analyst who makes profits from using candlestick patterns to analyze markets, hence the need for you to spot profitable candlestick patterns at a glance using the different types of candlestick patterns. At this point, I expect that when you hear terms like the morning star, bulling engulfing, hammer, inverted hammer, piercing line, and so on, you would quickly identify them as high probability candlestick patterns. You should also be able to identify bearish reversal candlestick patterns when you see them. Buy and sell techniques are also a useful part of candlestick analysis which you must have learned from reading this book.

From learning about technical analysis price patterns, we proceeded to learn about how to use candlestick charts to spot trends using variables like trend lines, trend following, and so on. By now you should be able to identify false breakouts for what they are, with the help of candlesticks.

This book closes with a banger on the last chapter which presents you with a cheat sheet that unravels the top candlestick secrets as well as the common mistakes to avoid when trading with candlestick patterns.

I am greatly confident in the fact that you now have everything you need to navigate through the hitherto stormy waters of market analysis especially when it comes to using candlesticks as a tool. Now that you have everything that you need, I hope that you use them as best as you can to become a master in whichever trade you wish to apply this knowledge. I am rooting for you and I hope that you share your experience to help others by leaving a review on Amazon.

References

Abhijit P. 2017. Candlestick Chart - Basic Anatomy. Retrieved from https://www.youtube.com/watch?v=_sQkh4acQhs

Alan F. 2021. The 5 Most Powerful Candlestick Patterns. Retrieved from https://www.investopedia.com/articles/active-trading/092315/5-most-powerful-candlestic k-patterns.asp

Alex O. N/D. Forex Candlestick Patterns Guide. Retrieved from https://www.fxstreet.com/rates-charts/chart/candlestick-patterns

Anne S. 2019. What is Technical Analysis? Definition, Basics and Examples. Retrieved from https://www.thestreet.com/investing/technical-analysis-14920339

Anzél K. 2020. How To Trade Using The Inverted Hammer Candlestick Pattern. https://www.ig.com/us/trading-strategies/how-to-trade-using-the-inverted-hammer-candl estick-pattern-191009#:~:text=The%20inverted%20hammer%20candlestick%20pattern %20(or%20inverse%20hammer)%20is%20a,downtrend%2C%20signalling%20poten tial %20bullish%20reversal.

Austin W. 2021. Candlestick Trading for Maximum Profits. Retrieved from https://www.dothefinancial.info/candlestick-charts.html

Bales K. 1993. Bulls and Bears Get Rich; the Goofy Don't : A Look at Buyers'

Psychology. Retrieved from

https://www.nytimes.com/1993/05/22/your-money/IHT-bulls-and-bears-get-rich-the-goofy-dont-a-look-at-buyers.html

Bennet J. 2016. 5 Trading Mistakes That Are Killing Your Profits + Simple Fixes. Retrieved from https://dailypriceaction.com/blog/technical-trading-mistakes/

Bigalow S. N/D. Major Candlestick Signals: 12 Signals to Master Any Market. Retrieved from

http://stephenbigalow.com/pdfs/MajorSignals.pdf?inf_contact_key=3485a6ad8af13b b91_03be467fedc3897184ddf05a406a093bd68350ff985e728

Binance Academy 2021. 12 Popular Candlestick Patterns Used in Technical Analysis. Retrieved from https://academy.binance.com/en/articles/beginners-candlestick-patterns

Broking A. 2020. Intraday Candlestick Chart Patterns. Retrieved from https://www.angelbroking.com/knowledge-center/share-market/intraday-chart-patterns

Chartformations.com 2020. The Morning Star. Retrieved from http://www.chart-formations.com/candlestick-patterns/morning-star.aspx

Cmegroup.com N/D. Fundamental Analysis vs Technical Analysis. Retrieved from https://www.cmegroup.com/education/courses/technical-analysis/fundamental-analysis-vs-technical-analysis.html

Coinloop 2018. The 4 Steps to Conquering Technical Analysis (Beginners Guide). Retrieved from

https://medium.com/@coinloop/the-4-steps-to-conquering-technical-analysis-beginners-guide-b4c90340a4b8

Corey M. 2021. Hammer Candlestick. Retrieved from https://www.investopedia.com/terms/h/hammer.asp

Corey M. 2020. Bearish Engulfing Pattern Definition and Tactics. Retrieved from https://www.investopedia.com/terms/b/bearishengulfingp.asp#:~:text=A%20bearish %20engulfing%20pattern%20is,engulfs%22%20the%20smaller%20up%20candle.

Corporate Finance Institute (n.d). Bull vs Bear. Retrieved from https://corporatefinanceinstitute.com/resources/knowledge/trading-investing/bull-vs-bear /

Dailyfx.com N/D. Candlestick Patterns. Retrieved from https://www.dailyfx.com/education/candlestick-patterns

Damyan D. 2020. N/D How to Read Candlestick Charts. Retrieved from
https://www.benzinga.com/money/how-to-read-candlestick-charts/#bullish-vs.-
bearish-c andles

Day Trading Encyclopedia. Candlestick Charts, History Of Candlestick Charts.
Retrieved from https://www.investorsunderground.com/stock-charts/candlestick-
charts/

Daytrading.com N/D Trading Patterns. Retrieved from
https://www.daytrading.com/patterns

Easy Markets. N/D. Identifying Candlestick Patterns and Momentum. Retrieved from
https://www.easymarkets.com/int/learn-centre/understanding-analysis/identifying-
candle stick-patterns-and-momentum/

Elearnmarkets 2021. 5 Powerful Bullish Candlestick Patterns. Retrieved from
https://www.elearnmarkets.com/blog/5-powerful-bullish-candlestick-patterns/

Elearnmarkets 2020. How to Trade with Inverted Hammer: Candlestick Pattern.

Retrieved from

https://www.elearnmarkets.com/blog/how-to-trade-with-inverted-hammer-
candlestick-pattern/

Eric R. 2021 Technical Analysis vs. Fundamental Analysis. Retrieved from
https://investorjunkie.com/investing/what-is-technical-analysis-vs-fundamental-
analysis/

Farley A. 2021. The 5 Most Powerful Candlestick Patterns. Retrieved from
https://www.investopedia.com/articles/active-trading/092315/5-most-powerful-
candlestic k-patterns.asp

Forextraders.com N/D. The Bullish Piercing Line Candlestick Chart Pattern.
https://www.forextraders.com/forex-education/forex-technical-analysis/the-bullish-
piercin g-line-candlestick-chart-pattern/

Forex Training Group N/D. Learn How to Read Forex Candlestick Charts Like a Pro.
Retrieved from

https://forextraininggroup.com/learn-read-forex-candlestick-charts-like-pro/

Galstyan M. 2021. Using Bullish Candlestick Patterns To Buy Stocks. Retrieved from https://www.investopedia.com/articles/active-trading/062315/using-bullish-candlestick-p atterns-buy-stocks.asp

Gordon C. 2020. Piercing Pattern. Retrieved from https://www.investopedia.com/terms/piercing-pattern.asp

Groww.in N/D. Difference between Fundamental and Technical Analysis. Retrieved from https://groww.in/p/difference-between-fundamental-and-technical-analysis/

Harry N. 2018. The 5 Most Effective Risk Management Techniques that the Pros Use.

Retrieved from

https://harrynicholls.medium.com/the-5-most-effective-risk-management-techniques-that-the-pros-use-a3bf7191f682

Humbled Trader. 2020. TOP 5 Day Trading Beginner Mistakes to AVOID. Retrieved from https://www.youtube.com/watch?v=CRPHmftchxU

Ig.com N/D. A Trader's Guide To The Three White Soldiers Candlestick Pattern. https://www.ig.com/en/trading-strategies/a-trader_s-guide-to-the-three-white-soldiers-ca ndlestick-pattern-200218

Ig.com 2020. 16 candlestick patterns every trader should know. Retrieved from https://www.ig.com/en/trading-strategies/16-candlestick-patterns-every-trader-should-kn ow-180615

Keydifferences.com 2019. Difference Between Fundamental and Technical Analysis.

Retrieved from

https://keydifferences.com/difference-between-fundamental-and-technical-analysis.html

James C. 2021. Guide to Technical Analysis. Retrieved from https://www.investopedia.com/terms/t/technical-analysis-of-stocks-and-trends.asp

James C. 2021. Bullish Engulfing Pattern. Retrieved from
https://www.investopedia.com/terms/b/bullishengulfingpattern.asp

James C. 2020. Morning Star Definition. Retrieved from
https://www.investopedia.com/terms/m/morningstar.asp

Justin B. 2015. How to Trade the Bullish Engulfing Pattern. Retrieved from
https://dailypriceaction.com/blog/how-to-trade-the-bullish-engulfing-pattern/

Justin K., 2021. Risk Management Techniques for Active Traders. Retrieved from
https://www.investopedia.com/articles/trading/09/risk-management.asp

Lawrence P. 2021. How To Use An Inverted Hammer Candlestick Pattern In
Technical Analysis. Retrieved from https://commodity.com/technical-
analysis/inverted-hammer/

Manish H. 2020. Debunking the Myths of Technical Analysis. Retrieved from
https://www.grazia.co.in/lifestyle/debunking-the-myths-of-technical-analysis-
5796.html

Marianna G. 2021. Using Bullish Candlestick Patterns To Buy Stocks. Retrieved
from https://www.investopedia.com/articles/active-trading/062315/using-bullish-
candlestick-p atterns-buy-stocks.asp

**Melissa H. 2021. When to Use Fundamental, Technical, and Quantitative
Analysis:**

These 3 methods help you evaluate long-term investments. Retrieved from
https://www.investopedia.com/ask/answers/050515/it-better-use-fundamental-
analysis-t echnical-analysis-or-quantitative-analysis-evaluate-
longterm.asp#:~:text=Technical%20
analysis%20uses%20data%20from,on%20information%20that%20spans%20years.

Milton A. 2021. How to Read a Candlestick Chart. Retrieved from
https://www.thebalance.com/how-to-read-a-candlestick-chart-1031115

Mitchel C. 2021. Understanding Basic Candlestick Charts. Retrieved from
https://www.investopedia.com/trading/candlestick-charting-what-is-
it/?utm_term=12230600&utm_campaign=www.investopedia.com&utm_medium=em

ail&utm_source=term-of-t he-day

Morris G. 2006. Candlestick Charting Explained (3rd Edition). Retrieved from
https://store.stockcharts.com/products/candlestick-charting-explained-3rd-edition

Nasdaq.com 2018. 5 Big Myths of Technical Analysis. Retrieved from
https://www.grazia.co.in/lifestyle/debunking-the-myths-of-technical-analysis-5796.html

Online Trading Academy. 2018. How to Read Candlestick Charts. Retrieved from
https://www.youtube.com/watch?v=FsqoV1aVrUc&t=5s

Picardo E. 2019. Common Investor and Trader Blunders. Retrieved from
https://www.investopedia.com/articles/active-trading/013015/worst-mistakes-beginner-tr aders-make.asp

Rayner T. 2020. The Hammer Candlestick Trading Strategy Guide.

https://www.tradingwithrayner.com/hammer-candlestick/

Rayner T. 2020. The Complete Guide to Candlestick Chart. Retrieved from
https://www.tradingwithrayner.com/candlestick-chart/

Rayner T. 2020. Sniper Trading Entries To Profit In Bull & Bear Markets (That Nobody Tells You). Retrieved from
https://www.youtube.com/watch?v=OrGChv83PDI

Richard B. 2019. Fundamental Vs. Technical Analysis – Beginner's Guide with Pros And Cons Of Each Investment Analysis Method. Retrieved from
https://catanacapital.com/blog/fundamental-vs-technical-analysis-beginners-guide/#fund amental-vs-technical-analysis

Rose M. N/D. Everything you wanted to know about candlestick charts. Retrieved from https://www.tradersclass.net/downloads/candlestickbook.pdf

School.stockcharts.com N/D. Technical Analysis. Retrieved from
https://school.stockcharts.com/doku.php?id=overview:technical_analysis#:~:text=Technical%20Analysis%20is%20the%20forecasting,examination%20of%20past%20price%20movements.&text=Technical%20analysis%20is%20applicable%20to,forces%2

0of%20s upply%20and%20demand.

Seth S. 2021. Technical Analysis Strategies for Beginners. Retrieved from https://www.investopedia.com/articles/active-trading/102914/technical-analysis-strategie s-beginners.asp

Seth S. (2020). Debunking 8 Myths About Technical Analysis. Retrieved from https://www.investopedia.com/articles/active-trading/062215/debunking-8-myths-about-t echnical-analysis.asp

Tradecity.com N/D. 9 Tips That Will Improve Your Risk Management Right Now. Retrieved from http://tradeciety.com/why-most-traders-lose-money-risk-management/

Tradingstrategyguides.com 2020. How to Build a Trading Risk Management Strategy. Retrieved from https://tradingstrategyguides.com/trading-risk-management-strategy/

Venketas W. 2019. 10 Trading Mistakes to Avoid in Forex Trading. Retrieved from https://www.dailyfx.com/education/find-your-trading-style/trading-mistakes.html

Vitalis I. 2019. 10 Most Common Trading Mistakes You Should Avoid. Retrieved from https://news.tradimo.com/10-most-common-trading-mistakes-you-should-avoid/

Warren V. 2019. How to Trade with the Piercing Line Pattern. Retrieved from https://www.dailyfx.com/education/candlestick-patterns/piercing-pattern.html

Warren V. 2019. Trading the Bullish Hammer Candle. https://www.dailyfx.com/education/candlestick-patterns/bullish-hammer.html

Wh S. 2020. 8 Wrong Myth about Technical Analysis in the Capital Market, Is it Right? Retrieved from https://julizar.id/en/blog/wrong-myth-technical-analysis